UNSHAKEABLE

When Life Falls Apart, You Don't Have To

By Kathy Kirk

Copyright © 2025 Kathy Kirk
All rights reserved.

No part of this publication may be reproduced, stored in a retrieval system, or transmitted in any form or by any means—electronic, mechanical, photocopying, recording, or otherwise—without prior written permission of the author, except in the case of brief quotations used in reviews and articles.

ISBN:
Hardcover: 979-8-9987731-0-5
Paperback: 979-8-9987731-1-2

Scripture quotations are taken from the Holy Bible, New King James Version®, unless otherwise noted. Copyright © 1982 by Thomas Nelson. Used by permission. All rights reserved.

This book is a work of nonfiction. Names and personal stories shared with permission have been used to illustrate biblical truths. Any similarity to persons living or dead, beyond the author's intention, is purely coincidental.

Cover design by M.A. Rehman
Printed in the United States of America
First Edition: 2025

Kathykirk.org
www.amazon.com/author/kathykirk

Dedication

First and foremost, I give all thanks to the Lord—who enabled, graced, and provided everything needed to write this book. Without Him, this would not exist.

To my Dad—
Everything I am today, and anything I will ever do, is because of you. You preserved me. You placed me on the path that would forever guide my life—the path of knowing my heavenly Father. I will forever be grateful. And you were the epitome of being Unshakeable. Thank you for showing me how to be such. I love you so deeply, Dad.

To my sister, Lisa—
Your courage, stoic tenacity, and quiet strength inspire me endlessly. You are an incredible mother, sister, wife, and daughter. I am beyond honored to have you in my life. You've encouraged me to keep going when I was at my lowest, and you've always believed in me. You, also, have mirrored the definition of Unshakeable. Thank you for being my constant.

UNSHAKEABLE
Table of Contents

1. Introduction 1
2. The Diagnosis That Changed Everything... 6
3. What the Test Didn't Reveal................. 10
4. Born to Be Unshakeable...................... 16
5. Disarm the Enemy – Resist Fear............ 21
6. You Are Not the Victim...................... 31
7. God Wants to Talk to You................... 43
8. Hearing God in the Storm................... 49
9. How to Hear God in Everyday Life......... 59
10. Shut Thy Mouth… And Open It............ 77
11. The Set Up..................................... 87
12. Power in Proactivity......................... 96
13. Don't Panic – Turn Inside................... 105
14. The Waiting Period or the Weighting Period?... 111
15. The Mind of a Champion................... 125
16. He Will Show You............................ 140
17. Jehovah Shammah........................... 152
18. What to Do When You Don't Know What to Do... 170
19. Jurassic Park – Your Fence Is Your Best Defense... 183
20. Peace When Everything Falls Apart........ 195
21. You've Got the Victory...................... 201
22. Hold On… And Let Go..................... 213
23. Prayer to Receive Jesus as Lord............ 215
24. Prayer to Receive the Baptism of the Holy Spirit.. 216
25. Acknowledgments........................... 217
26. About the Author............................ 218

Introduction

It was April 11, 1965—Palm Sunday in West Michigan. The sun was shining, and the spring air was filled with hope. Families gathered for dinners, birthday celebrations, and scenic countryside drives. After a long, bitter winter, joy and renewal seemed to be breaking through.

But in a sudden twist, everything changed.

Monster-sized tornadoes swept through the region with no time to prepare. Devastation hit hard and fast, claiming the lives of 50 people and leaving many others stunned and broken.

The tornado didn't care that people were enjoying a rare warm day with their families. It didn't wait for a more convenient time. It struck anyway because life doesn't wait until you're ready.

That's what a bad report feels like.

Maybe your storm didn't come from the sky but from a phone call or a diagnosis. Perhaps it hit while you were decorating a birthday cake… driving to work… watching your child play a baseball game… or in the middle of a Sunday nap.

Whatever the setting, the result was the same — shock, fear, confusion.

Unshakeable: Standing Firm When Life Falls Apart

Most of us remember that moment—the day the bad news came. The phone rang. The diagnosis was spoken. The ground beneath your life shifted.

And just like that, you were in the middle of a storm. A whirlwind of fear, confusion, and uncertainty followed, leaving you gasping for peace and clarity in the chaos.

I know that place. I've been there—in the middle of a tragedy. In the moment that stops you. A moment that changes your plans, shakes your confidence, and makes you wonder, *What now?*

I remember one Christmas, just after the holidays, my mom ended up in the hospital with COVID. We had just shared some of the most beautiful moments—conversations at the outdoor café in Galveston, shopping in boutiques, dinner at her favorite restaurant in Houston, and lunch at our favorite tea house. Sweet memories of that Christmas I'll always cherish.

Then everything flipped.

From that hospital in Texas, she texted me saying she didn't think she was going to live through this—and gave me her attorney's name in case she died.

I broke. I panicked. I wept.

I couldn't get to her. My sister and others in our family were sick too, also with COVID. I thought about flying home to Texas to see her in the hospital—but I had COVID as well.

But after I unraveled... I got back up.

I forced myself to put emotions aside, take my position in Christ as a victor, and refuse to accept defeat through panic or fear.

I reached for what *I knew*. The tools God had already given me as a covenant child. And I started using them.

I picked up the Word. I began speaking healing Scriptures over her body—three times a day—because God's Word is, "...*life* to all that find them and health to all their flesh." (Proverbs 4:22). I became her spiritual nurse, feeding her God's medicine.

I declared healing. I stood in faith. I reminded myself: *There's no distance in prayer.*

The good news? *God brought her through. Healed. Whole. No residue.*

That's what being Unshakeable looks like.

When starting to write this book, my thinking was that it would be a short guide—a survival manual for how to respond when the worst happens. But the more I wrote, the more I realized something deeper:

Being Unshakeable isn't just about what to do when the storm hits—it's about how to live before it ever does. And, it's about how to stay standing strong while you're still in the storm.

Because sometimes, when bad news comes, it's too late to figure out what you believe.

And other times, you get hit in the middle of the mess, needing help right now.

That's what this book is for.

It's for the moments when life doesn't make sense—and the moments before those moments.

Because bad news comes. Storms hit. Sometimes they knock us off our feet—at least for a moment. But that doesn't have to be the end of your story.

This book will help you know what to do when the ground shakes. How to respond in faith and not react in fear. To know how to rise when the wind gets knocked out of you.

To hear God clearly in the middle of the crisis. How to stand when everything around you is telling you to collapse. To recognize God's peace when panic tries to take hold.

You'll find real stories, spiritual tools, and biblical truths to help you fight back in faith and stay grounded in complete assurance and confidence.

This isn't just encouragement—it's a guide map for the storm. A how-to on standing when life tries to throw you flat.

It's about passing through the fire without being consumed. It's about staying positioned for victory—refusing to be shaken, silenced or taken out.

You may not be able to stop the storm, but you can stand through it. You can hold your peace when others lose theirs. You can be steady when life falls apart. You can be confident, assured and hopeful, knowing that the God of the Universe is on *your* side.

Whether you're facing a crisis right now...Or you want to be emotionally and spiritually ready for whatever life brings—

This book is for you.

You can be Unshakeable.

The Diagnosis That Changed Everything

"We saw a mass...you'll need to come back in for more testing."

Following a routine yearly physical, the letter from my doctor began with positivity—but ended with that unsettling last paragraph. My mind started racing, but I brushed the thoughts aside and called the office for a follow-up appointment. Before I could even get through, the hospital called me.

I kept my composure on the phone as the receptionist scheduled a date for more testing. Outwardly, I remained calm. Inwardly, thoughts swirled. *What if?* Years ago, I had cancer in this same area. Could it be back?

Memories rushed in. The last time I'd heard the words *"come back for further examination,"* it *had* been cancer. I thought of people I knew who had survived cancer only to have it return years later. My emotions wanted to run ahead, but I made a decision: **I would stay in control.** I wouldn't speak of this to anyone—not my family, brother (a physician), friends, or prayer team. Not even my pastor. Just me and the Father.

Since faith works by love, I knew my first step was to check my heart. I asked the Holy Spirit *if there was any unforgiveness or bitterness hiding in me. How's my love walk? Did I open the door somewhere?* After some time in prayer and shutting down the noise in my mind, peace came. It was the kind of peace that settles deep in your spirit and whispers, *"Everything is going to be okay."* Hallelujah!

The follow-up appointment wasn't scheduled for another three weeks. In the meantime, life stayed busy—work, travel, ministry. Even so, I remained intentional about meditating on healing scriptures, confessing God's Word, and feeding my spirit with truth.

But gradually—subtly—the enemy crept in.

Without realizing it, during that "waiting period," thoughts began to slip in: *What if the results aren't favorable? What if this alters the momentum in my life if it is cancer? What if it's aggressive or spreading?* These thoughts didn't bombard me all at once. They came in little spurts—just enough to plant seeds. I didn't notice it at first because I was so busy. But over time, those thoughts bore fruit—concern, heaviness, and a quiet erosion of peace.

The enemy is persistent. One afternoon, standing at the kitchen sink rinsing a plate, suddenly the thought settled in: *"Just accept it, that cancer came back, don't fight it, it will be fine, just like the last time."*

When I was diagnosed with cancer years back, I had just returned to the Lord after a long, backslidden season. And yet, God's faithfulness was astounding. The cancer was caught early—it was at grade zero. My insurance covered my medical and hospital bills *and* a naturopathic doctor—the latter that my company *stopped* covering the very next year. My treatment schedule was ideal. The side effects were minimal. Even the parking at this vast hospital was easy! God had walked with me every step, providing grace and favor in every detail.

With the thoughts that day in the kitchen came a strange calm, like an invitation to surrender.

Not the kind of surrender that brings healing or trust, but the type that sounds wise...while leading you away from the truth. The more I stood there, the more reasonable it all seemed. But thank God for the Spirit within me—despite the temptation to secede, I knew this was not of God. That was not my Shepherd's voice, although it was well mimicked. It was a counterfeit calm meant to lure me into agreement. It sounded reasonable, even comforting.

But it was a trap—a setup.

The enemy disguised his voice to sound like peace. He often poses as an angel of light (2 Corinthians 11:14). The Bible also says to test the spirits (I John 4:1). That's why it's so vital to know the Word—what the Bible says—so we don't get deceived by emotions or "feelings" that contradict truth. If an experience—even a sense of peace—doesn't align with the Word of God, the Bible, it must be rejected. The Word is the final authority.

II Corinthians 11:14
14 And no marvel; for Satan himself is transformed into an angel of light.

I John 4:1
1 Beloved, believe not every spirit, but try the spirits whether they are of God: because many false prophets are gone out into the world.

That day in the kitchen, I realized what was happening. I rebuked the enemy and boldly stood on the truth of who I am in Christ—because of what Jesus did for me. I will not accept anything that the enemy has to offer, especially when Jesus paid such a high and terrible price to redeem me.

As the appointment approached for the extra testing—now only days away and falling the day *before* my birthday—I still didn't feel settled. My birthday usually brings great joy, but instead, it seemed to intensify the concerns. I had stayed in the Word, confessed healing scriptures, and done all the "right" things.

So why wasn't I walking in peace?

Why wasn't I experiencing that deep assurance I knew was mine in Christ?

Lord, what's wrong? This isn't normal. You promise peace that passes understanding, especially in uncertain times—but I'm not walking in it. Why?

During our church worship service one Sunday, I was lost in worship, sensing the Lord's sweet presence yet feeling conflicted. He was talking to me about my calling and future—and I wanted to interrupt Him. Why was He talking to me about my future? Doesn't He understand what is ahead? I wanted to say, "Lord, don't You see what's coming up this week? I need You to talk about *that*." I needed His reassurance and His Word on it. But He didn't say anything. And it wasn't silence out of neglect—it was peace out of knowing. From His vantage point, this wasn't even a matter worth discussing. It was already done. It was as if He was saying, "Why would I speak to fear when I've already given you truth?" I was giving more attention to what the enemy was doing, and the Lord took no notice.

None at all, in fact, none whatsoever. He didn't bring it up, not one word. And that puzzled me. I knew the Lord knew, but why wasn't he commenting on this?

And honestly? That made me ponder more.

Why was *I* so anxious while *He* seemed so calm?

Something just wasn't right. I had experienced that supernatural peace before in tough times, but it was not there this time.

That night, still feeling off, I finally confessed something out loud in prayer—something I hadn't fully admitted to myself. I don't think I ever realized it until all the noise was shut off, and in my desire to have that confidence, I was seeking God. In the search, I finally said it.

"Lord...I'm afraid."

There it was—the missing link, the unseen thread behind the lack of peace, the diagnosis that changed everything.

Fear had crept in—quiet, cunning, disguised as logic and busyness—and stolen my peace.

But naming it wasn't the end. I still had one more step.

And that's what I discovered next.

And that's precisely what happened... *What the Test Didn't Reveal.*

What the Test Didn't Reveal

"Fear!"

That was the word the Lord whispered clearly to my heart that morning of the appointment.

The Holy Spirit continued, *"You were in fear. You allowed fear to come in."*

I wondered why, despite confessing healing scriptures and standing on God's Word, I wasn't experiencing the peace I knew was mine. That quiet response from the Lord answered everything. It was simple—yet powerful.

You let fear in.

That's why the peace that had anchored me early on was no longer active. God's woman of faith and power, ready to conquer the world—and yet unknowingly entertaining fear for weeks. How had I missed it?

But that's the thing about fear. It rarely barges in with sirens blaring. It sneaks in through reasoning, feelings, and subtle suggestions. Thank God for the Holy Spirit, our Helper. He leads us into all truth and gives us wisdom when we ask. As children of God, there is no reason to walk through life not knowing.

James 1:5-7
5 *If any man lack wisdom, let him ask of God, who giveth to all men liberally, and upbraideth not; and it shall be given him.*

6 But let him ask in faith, nothing wavering, for he that wavereth is like a wave of the sea driven with the wind and tossed.
7 For let not that man think that he shall receive anything of the Lord.

Jesus said in John 8:32 that *"And you shall know the truth, and the truth shall make you free."* The Holy Spirit leads us into all truth, and that truth sets us free.

John 16:13
13 Howbeit when he, the Spirit of truth, is come, he will guide you into all truth; for he shall not speak of himself, but whatsoever he shall hear, that shall he speak: and he will shew you things to come.

That's precisely what He did. He showed me. The same morning as my follow-up appointment—I got up, made coffee, and sat quietly with the Lord. That's when He spoke about what I had been trying to uncover for weeks.

"You're in fear."

And in that moment, everything made sense. His answer was simple. It's so simple that I'm almost embarrassed to admit how long I missed it.

But that's why I'm writing this book.

Instantly, the heaviness lifted. The anointing returned like a cloak around me. Peace rushed in, and assurance stood guard.

When he showed me the real enemy—fear—I knew exactly what to do. I repented for allowing it in. Then, I resisted it and commanded it to go in Jesus' name. *Fear is a spirit.* And when rebuked in Jesus' name, it cannot stay.

At this point, it was no longer about the testing results—it was about keeping fear out. That was the *real* battle.

And here's the truth: you have authority over fear. Jesus gave it to you. You are a covenant child of a covenant God. You sit in heavenly places with Christ—fear is under your feet! It has no right to dominate your thoughts, decisions, or emotions.

On the way to the hospital, I wasn't worried, tense, or at peace. Walking through the familiar building where I had received treatment years ago, I passed patients who were undergoing care. A thought tried to sneak in: *"That could be you."*

But thoughts don't win unless we let them stay.

We choose what stays in our minds. We stand at the door of our thought life and decide what gets to live there. I quietly spoke under my breath at that moment, addressing fear directly. I refused to agree with it. I didn't even bother rebuking sickness—because that wasn't the issue.

Fear was.

(And that's a vital point we'll explore in another chapter.)

After checking in, I sat in the waiting area with a few others. A woman came out from one of the doors and rushed to her mom, embracing her and saying, "Everything came back normal!" The wave of relief in her voice told the story—fear had gripped her before that news. It was a reminder that fear is a standard weapon the enemy uses.

Soon, the room cleared except for me and another woman. We struck up a casual conversation about life—nothing medical. But she repeated the exact phrase for every topic we touched on:

"It's scary. It's just really scary."

Over and over again, *"It's scary."*

I smiled, but I didn't say much. I wasn't going to agree with fear—not even in conversation. The agreement gives fear permission. And I had already decided—*fear was not allowed back in.*

When the tests were done and the results returned that morning, they were negative.

My reaction? Nothing dramatic.

Why?

Because after fear was removed, peace was in place. The results didn't define the moment—peace did. The real victory wasn't in the outcome. The real triumph was in keeping fear out and refusing to give the enemy an open door to wreak havoc through worry, dread, and intimidation.

When a bad report comes—or even the threat of one—you can remain **Unshakeable** by resisting fear first and foremost.

Someone once told me, "That sounds good on paper, but it's impossible not to be afraid in those moments." They added, *"It's normal to be afraid of the result."*

But…*is it?*

Is fear our normal for the born-again covenant child of a covenant God?

What does God's Word say?

We'll explore that in another chapter.

Born to Be Unshakeable

"Surely the righteous will never be shaken; they will be remembered forever. They will have no fear of bad news; their hearts are steadfast, trusting in the Lord."— Psalm 112:6–7

The definition of *Unshakeable* is *firm and unwavering*. It describes two entities: the object in the storm and the storm itself. The title *Unshakeable* belongs to the one still standing amid the storm—no matter how intense the wind, how high the water, or how fierce the fire. They might be drenched with water or covered in ashes, but still standing. Though the storm's nature and intent is to destroy and bring down, the Unshakeable one remains intact—radiating strength rooted in a foundation stronger than the storm's force or intent.

That is Unshakeable. *You were born to be Unshakeable.*

In 1972, the Fiji Islands faced the formidable Hurricane Bebe. Schools closed their doors, businesses paused, and authorities rallied into neighborhoods with megaphones, encouraging everyone to seek shelter. The calm before the storm was unforgettable—it was a surreal stillness as the island braced itself. During this time, we lived in a charming flat on stilts while our home was under construction. This was our inaugural encounter with such a powerful hurricane, and it filled us with both trepidation and curiosity about what lay ahead. It was an experience that proved God's faithfulness towards his children and reminded us that no matter how strong the winds, we are rooted in something stronger. We are born to stand, born to win and born to be Unshakeable.

As the storm approached, we placed our animals in a small doghouse under the flat and hunkered down with the rest of Fiji. The storm arrived with speed and ferocity. Roofs were torn off homes and businesses, buildings collapsed, livestock were swept away, and trees were uprooted. Power lines snapped, unleashing nature's fury in one of Fiji's most powerful storms.

But not on us.

Not on our flat built on stilts. Although we could feel the flat sway back and forth, it did not succumb to the powerful, damaging winds. And that fragile doghouse where all our animals were sheltered remained untouched. Our neighbors' roofs flew off, and trees crashed around us, but we were safe.

As the water began to rise in the flat, we used every piece of linen we had to try to keep it out. We propped the furniture up on vegetable cans to prevent it from getting soaked. I remember watching my dad in the midst of it all—calm, unwavering, and steady.

As a child, watching him stand on the Word of God for our protection… was priceless. I had no fear. I felt safe because Dad wasn't panicking. He wasn't shaken.

He was…

Unshakeable.

A storm isn't just a weather event; it can be anything that unsettles us deeply and threatens what we hold most dear. It might be a grim doctor's report, a financial crisis, or an unexpected issue with our children.

Storms have the power to destroy, hinder, and stall progress. They bring feelings of intimidation, fear, uncertainty, and despair.

However, for those who remain Unshakeable, these storms do not spell defeat.

These are the moments in life when we're challenged—will we stand or fall, give in or fight, run or stay, believe or doubt, crumble or stabilize? We face storms that threaten our health, family, business, or future, but even amidst this uncertainty, we have a choice in how we respond.

Do we need to be victims of sudden bad news or fear-inducing reports, like "Hurricane Bebe" moments? No. When we remain steadfast, we hold on to what the enemy seeks to steal, including our identity. We are not victims overpowered by darkness; we are sons and daughters of God, equipped with divine power and spiritual tools. We are strong, focused, anointed, and powerful in the face of any attack from the enemy. If we want to gain new ground—and keep what is rightfully ours—we must be Unshakeable.

To be Unshakeable means standing firm in our faith when everything else is in flux.

It's trusting God's Word when your world doesn't make sense.

It's choosing truth even when your emotions scream otherwise.

It's declaring, *"God's Word is the final authority,"* even when the news isn't what you hoped for.

It's refusing to let fear write the headline for your day.

It's choosing to speak what God says—when everything else is shouting the opposite.

It's opening your mouth in prayer when all you want to do is shut down.

It's getting up the next day and choosing hope once again.

It's a steadfast determination to believe what God has promised—refusing to bow to intimidation or be broken by the battle.

In the fictional story of the three little pigs, each pig built a house: one made a house out of straw, another also made a house out of sticks, and the third pig built a house out of bricks. When the wolf came, he huffed and puffed and blew down the houses of the first two pigs. However, when he reached the third house made of bricks, he huffed and puffed but could not blow it down!

The foundation was strong; it was made of brick.

This concept is reflected in Matthew 7:24-27, where Jesus says:

24 Therefore, whoever hears these sayings of mine and does them, I will liken him to a wise man who built his house upon a rock.
25 And the rain descended, the floods came, and the winds blew and beat upon that house; and it did not fall, for it was founded upon a rock.

26 And everyone who hears these sayings of mine and does not do them will be likened to a foolish man who built his house upon the sand.
27 And the rain descended, the floods came, and the winds blew and beat upon that house; and it fell, and great was its fall.

Storms don't wait for the right moment; they come when they come. But you don't have to fear the forecast when you are rooted—when your life is built on the Rock of God's Word. You don't have to answer when despair calls. You don't have to crumble under pressure. And you don't have to give in to the belief that this will ruin you, break you, or define the rest of your life. With God's Word as a foundation, you will stand through it all, come out stronger, and be Unshakeable.

If we want to be Unshakeable, our foundation must be strong and built with the right ingredients.

That is why I wrote this book.

So that you can be **Unshakeable**—

When the winds rise, when the storm hits, when the pressure is on.

When Hurricane Bebe comes—literal or symbolic—you'll remember:

You were born to stand.
You were born to win.

        You were born to be **Unshakeable**.

Disarm The Enemy
Resist Fear

Leaving the hospital after the test, I called a close relative to share what God had shown me during these past weeks and the result of the test.

"I'm so glad everything's okay," she said. "But waiting for results with medical tests... it's hard not to be afraid."

I understood what she meant. She went on:

"It's normal to feel afraid sometimes—especially in situations like that."

Her words struck a chord. Fear may *feel* normal, but during my experience, I realized something powerful:

What feels natural isn't always harmless. Fear doesn't just trouble our minds—it's a weapon the enemy uses to undermine our faith, cloud our decisions, and steal our confidence.

Fear Is More Than a Feeling

To many, fear seems like a reasonable, even spiritual response. As I mentioned in my conversation with that relative, people often say, *"It's normal to be afraid... and God understands."*

That might sound comforting—but for a child of God, it's dangerous ground.

Fear is often the first response to bad news. And while it may be understandable it is also dangerous—because if fear is allowed to stay it will begin to lead. And fear is a terrible leader.

But fear isn't just an emotional response—it's also a spiritual tactic.

Fear is a strategy. Scripture tells us the enemy comes to steal, kill, and destroy (John 10:10). One of his most effective tactics is convincing us that fear is acceptable—that it's harmless and unavoidable. II Timothy 1:7 calls it the spirit of fear...but that spirit is not of God.

The Bible warns us not to be ignorant of Satan's schemes (2 Corinthians 2:11). When we allow fear to linger—when we tolerate it—we unknowingly give it power. We need to disarm the enemy.

Will we *feel* fear? Yes. But we don't have to accept it.

Fear Opens the Door...and Closes it

Fear can do both: It can open the door to the enemy and close the door to the miraculous.

We see this clearly in Job's story. Job was deeply devoted, yet his fear quietly compromised his faith. After devastating losses, he confessed:

"The thing which I greatly feared has come upon me" (Job 3:25).

Despite his sacrifices and prayers, Job's fear gave the enemy a legal opening. That's a sobering truth: even spiritual actions—like prayer or confession—can lose effectiveness if they're driven by fear rather than faith.

I've experienced this personally. There have been times I declared God's promises yet felt no peace. I rebuked sickness but still felt anxious. Why? Because my words were being fueled by fear, not anchored in faith.

Fear's Power to Paralyze

For many, fear can feel overwhelming—and impossible to control. When bad news arrives—whether a frightening diagnosis, a financial crisis, or a national tragedy—the natural response may be to panic. Fear comes with images and words and with that comes influence. But Jesus modeled a different way.

When Jairus received word that his daughter had died, Jesus immediately responded: *"Do not be afraid; only believe." (Mark 5:36).* Notice—Jesus didn't tell Jairus to start praying harder. He didn't instruct him to fast or start quoting scripture. He didn't ask him to speak to the mountain. No, the very first command He gave was simple and direct:

Resist fear.

Why? Jesus knew that before faith could rise, fear had to be confronted, and the enemy had to be disarmed.

After Jesus spoke to him, Jairus had the ability to resist fear and panic. We have the Greater One living within us, so we do not have to be victims of paralysis and panic.

There's a saying: "All you have to fear is fear itself." As children of God, we can turn that around: "All that fear has to fear is God Himself!" And God is in us! The Greater One lives on the inside of us. I John 4:4 says, "Ye are of God, little children, and have overcome them: because greater is he that is in you, than he that is in the world."

You can turn the tables. Fear is afraid of you when you know who you are in Christ and who is living on the inside of you. We do not have to succumb to fear and all of its counterparts, despair, intimidation or panic. No, we send them running!

So, when fear tries to dominate and intimidate, remember— the enemy knows who you are. If you know your identity in Christ, he is more afraid of you because of the God within you. That same power that allowed Jesus to defeat Satan and reclaim the keys to death, hell, and the grave is alive in you!

Understanding who you are and who resides in you will disarm the enemy in those moments. And when you know who you are, you can speak with authority and command fear to leave in the name of Jesus. *Speak to fear in Jesus's name and deny it entrance. Use your authority with your mouth. You have authority over fear.*

Fear's Hidden Tactics

Fear doesn't always announce its arrival. It creeps in quietly—like sugar hidden in processed foods—subtly affecting our decisions, our peace, and our outlook. One anxious thought, one unexpected moment, and suddenly, fear is everywhere. That's why identifying fear is so important.

When we recognize fear for what it truly is—a spiritual attack that we can confront it effectively and shut it down.

Common Triggers of Fear

Understanding what triggers fear can help us prepare for and stand against it. Here are a few common fear triggers:

- **Uncertain Outcomes** – Waiting on medical results, job decisions, or financial breakthroughs.
- **Sudden Crisis** – Emergencies, accidents, or breaking news.
- **Memories of Past Trauma** – Painful experiences that resurface during similar events.
- **Isolation** – Loneliness often intensifies anxious thoughts.

Recognizing these triggers ahead of time gives us a strategy. We can reinforce our hearts *before* fear strikes by arming ourselves with God's Word and anchoring our minds in His promises.

Disarm the Enemy: Bind the Strongman

Mark 3:27 reveals a vital principle:
"No one can enter a strongman's house and plunder his goods unless he first binds the strongman and then he will spoil his house."

In spiritual terms, fear is often the strongman. It must be resisted before God's promises take root in our hearts. When we rebuke fear, we disarm the enemy's hold—and allow faith to rise.

II Timothy 1:7 reminds us:
"God has not given us a spirit of fear, but of power, and of love, and a sound mind."

We don't have to yield to fear when a crisis hits. We have been given power, love, and a sound mind under pressure—love that never fails, the power that overcomes, and a sound mind that keeps us steady and clear—even when circumstances are chaotic.

These characteristics are our inheritance as children of God.

We can respond, not react hysterically. We have authority over fear—no matter how threatening the situation seems.

Resisting fear is the first step to standing firm and Unshakeable when bad news arrives. Disarm the enemy, resist fear first, and bind the strongman.

Rebuke Fear-Not Just the Problem

I once heard the story of a woman working in ministry. When her coworker left early one day, feeling sick, she immediately thought, *"I hope I don't get sick too."* Out of fear, she began rebuking sickness over herself.

But the next day—she woke up sick.

Why didn't her prayers seem to work? Because her motivation was fear. Instead of resisting fear first, she tried to fight the *symptoms*. The thought came, 'What if you get sick like that?' which elicited the response to rebuke symptoms out of fear instead of rebuking the fear.

We saw earlier how fear can creep in quietly. The enemy is subtle—he'll try to convince us to focus on a threat that hasn't even happened yet, like rebuking something that's not real while sneaking fear in through the back door.

Another woman spent years diligently praying against cancer. But despite all her prayers, she eventually received a diagnosis. Why? Because her prayers weren't coming from a place of faith. They were driven by fear—a fear that cancer would come. And that fear quietly took root, weakening her ability to rest in God's promises.

We can confess God's Word over ourselves, such as Psalm 91, Isa 53:4-5, and I Peter 2:24, and build on what the Word says instead of coming against something with fear. There is a difference.

Faith speaks with authority, while fear speaks with desperation. If we want to walk in absolute power and be unmovable, Unshakeable, we must address the fear first. Command fear to go.

It Begins in the Day to Day

Resisting fear is practiced in the day-to-day.

Earlier, we discussed how fear is like sugar—hidden in places we don't expect. It blends into our thoughts, choices, and routines so subtly that we don't always notice it.

But with the help of the Holy Spirit, we can begin to recognize these areas and train ourselves to use our authority—not just in moments of crisis but also in ordinary moments.

One time at church, our pastor was teaching during a meeting and asked for volunteers at the end to come up front and put the lesson into practice. I wanted to participate and learn, but fear held me back from participating.

I was intimidated and afraid. What if I failed? Or embarrassed myself? I didn't realize it, but afterward, I felt so disappointed. Fear had controlled my decision, and I hadn't even recognized it until it was over.

From then on, I resolved: Next time, I would use 2 Timothy 1:7. I would remind myself that I've been given *power, love, and a sound mind,* and not allowing fear to choose for me.

How many moments like that show up in our daily lives?

- The fear of asking your boss for a raise
- The fear of your child not coming home safely
- The fear of being honest with your spouse
- The fear of looking at the credit card bill
- The fear of being late for a meeting

Fear finds ways to slip in quietly when we're not paying attention. But once we start noticing it, we can resist it. We can shut the door on the enemy in the small things—so when a *big thing* comes, we're already trained to recognize it and disarm it.

If you deal with fear daily, you'll be equipped to overcome it in a crisis.

Practical Steps for Resisting Fear

Conquering fear isn't passive—it requires action. Here are a few practical steps to help you stand firm:

Identify Fear's Source: Ask the Holy Spirit to reveal where fear has taken root. Is it tied to health, finances, relationships, or the unknown? Maybe you have been cured of a disease and you quietly fear that it will come back or a relationship failed and there is fear that you will never find love again. The Holy Spirit will show you these areas.

Practice Rebuking Fear Immediately: Speak to fear with your mouth. Don't entertain fearful thoughts. Speak with authority in Jesus' name and command fear to leave. Thoughts will not resist fear, we need to speak to it.

Turn off Fear-Feeding Channels: Limit exposure to adverse reports that feed fear. This includes movies, too much news, and what you read or the music you listen to. Replace it with faith filled teachings, books, music. Here's the deal – what you put in your spirit, through what you feed on through your eyes or your ears is exactly what will come out in times of crisis. And even before a crisis – fear will envelope your life, your choices, your decisions, instead of faith. It is vitally important what we are listening to or watching.

Get Fear Out Of Your Mouth: Stop speaking fear-filled words like "I'm so afraid of…" or "That scares me to death." Start speaking God's Words like "God has not given me a spirit of fear, but of love, power and a sound mind", or "I am more than a conqueror through Him who loved me." Watch what you say and **refuse to confess** that fear rules in your life. When you confess God's Words, your spirit hears it and your mind hears it and you will start believing what you say!

Choosing Faith Over Fear

Resisting fear isn't a one-time decision—it's a daily mindset. That mindset prepares you to stand firm when life's storms come.

As you grow in that mindset, you won't just experience peace for yourself—you'll become a steadying presence for those around you. In a world of fear, your courage will point others to our Unshakeable hope in Jesus.

The next time fear rises, remember: You can stop it. Living without fear isn't about denying reality or pretending problems don't exist. It's about responding differently. It's about recognizing fear's tactics—and choosing to resist them in Jesus' name.

Panic is not your only option. Breakdown is not your only outcome.

Victory is possible. But it begins with resisting fear.

Fear has no place in the life of a child of God. Bind the strongman first—and you'll find the strength to stand, no matter the challenge. Each of us will face moments that test our faith. But when we resist fear, we stop the enemy from gaining ground.

Let's make a firm decision today: to stand in faith, to take our place of authority, and to refuse to be ruled by fear—not in daily decisions and not in crisis.

Disarm the enemy. Resist Fear. Be Unshakeable.

You Are Not the Victim!

You may have been hurt. Lied to. Knocked down. But you were never created to stay there. You are not what happened to you — you are who God says you are.

What gives someone a victim mentality? What separates the person who believes they'll never recover — especially when crisis or tragedy strikes — from the one who rises and conquers?

It all comes down to what they believe.

In this chapter, I want to help you rewrite the internal story shaping how you see yourself — so you can walk in the Unshakeable victory Jesus died to give you. Because when the enemy throws his best shot, you don't have to collapse into a powerless identity. You were born to rise. To stand. To overcome.

Our beliefs are often shaped by experience—especially by how we interpret those experiences. Those moments can leave deep marks if we've gone through hard times, particularly during childhood—a vulnerable and formative season.

When abuse, rejection, or abandonment strike and we have no power to rescue ourselves, it's easy to carry that sense of helplessness into adulthood. We begin to believe that we are powerless and always will be. There will always be someone or something stronger, smarter, or more dominant that wins…while we lose.

That belief becomes our internal truth. It's real. Raw. And often reinforced by years of disappointment and defeat.

We begin to believe that *I'm the victim. I always have been. I always will be.*

But why do we hold onto that belief?

If you find yourself constantly looking for pity, waiting for someone to rescue you, or replaying your hardships on a loop—it may be time to check your mindset. You might be stuck in a victim narrative. But the good news? You don't have to stay there. Jesus has already given you the victory—and it's time to live like it.

For many of us no one ever taught us how to live any differently. So when hard times come again, we default to the only narrative we've ever known. The voice of defeat can sound like this:

"This will overcome you too."
"This situation is more powerful than you—just like the others."
"You can try to fight, but it's stronger."
"You don't have what it takes."
After all… you're a victim. Aren't you?

Here's the hard truth:
Sometimes, we get so used to living with the enemy that we stop fighting altogether.

We become accustomed to it. We don't know how to fight it—so we survive it. We endure because we've never seen a way out. We're always waiting for someone to rescue us—yet Jesus already has.

This is how strongholds are formed: mental and emotional fortresses built from repeated thoughts and reinforced lies. They shape our view of life, ourselves, and even God. They determine who we believe has power—and who doesn't.

And the real danger? We start letting our circumstances define us, our future, our relationships, our identity and even how we see life.

Change the Default

But truth be told—the power lies within you. Past defeats, abuse, or painful experiences do not get to decide who holds the power *now*.

You do.

What happened in the past doesn't have the right to dictate who wins the war today—or who keeps winning. It doesn't have that authority... *unless you permit it.*

The difference between a victim and a victor often comes down to one simple thing:

What you believe.

"As a man thinketh in his heart, so is he."— *Proverbs 23:7*

It's not what *has happened* or even what *is happening* that defines who you are. It's what you believe.

If you want to shift from victim to victor, it starts with confronting your belief system.

If you want to walk through life with confidence, strength, and authority—conquering the battles that come your way—you must change the default.

Some beliefs are so deeply rooted that they feel like part of us. But in reality, they're strongholds—fortresses of thought built by lies we've unknowingly accepted.

Strongholds don't break on their own. They are dismantled by truth. And that truth comes from one place: God's Word.

Jesus didn't just save you—He empowered you.

"Behold, I give you power to tread upon serpents and scorpions, and over all the power of the enemy, and nothing shall by any means hurt you."— Luke 10:19

Only you can choose what you believe and change your internal script. But you have the power and the ability to do so.

Changing the default doesn't happen in one big moment. It's choosing to respond differently in a familiar situation. It's recognizing when fear rises—and speaking the truth instead. It's catching yourself when the old narrative plays and saying, *"That's not who I am anymore."*

Maybe the old default said, *"You'll always be rejected."*
Now, the truth says, *"I am accepted in the Beloved."*
Maybe the default said, *"You're not strong enough."*
The truth says, *"I am strong in the Lord, and the power of His might."*

Little by little, those defaults get rewritten. Truth gets louder than the lies.

Say it out loud. Speak God's Word. Write it down. Stand in front of the mirror and remind yourself:

I am not a victim. I am victorious in Christ.
You are not bound. You are not beneath. You are not broken beyond repair.

You are chosen. You are strong. You are free. You are Unshakeable in Him.

Rewrite Your Story

Remember the rhyme, *Humpty Dumpty?* The best loved rhyme about an egg.

> Humpty Dumpty sat on a wall
> Humpty Dumpty had a great fall
> All the king's horses and all the king's men
> Couldn't put Humpty Dumpty back together again!

Perhaps you can relate to that broken egg—and the enemy has you deceived into thinking that you cannot rewrite your story. There have been too many broken expectations, dreams, and hearts. That's totally reasonable. Life can hit hard.

However, let's see what God's Word says:
"Though the righteous fall seven times, they rise again." — Proverbs 24:16

Joseph, David, Jesus, Paul, and many others in the Bible were knocked down and counted out—but they rose again. They didn't let what had happened to them become the final chapter. And just like them, through Christ, you can rewrite your story with your new identity. Jesus has already given you the pen and the paper—and He wrote the last chapter. And… you win.

If Humpty Dumpty's story had been rewritten, it might have ended like this:

> Humpty Dumpty sat on a wall
> Humpty Dumpty had a great fall
> All the king's horses and all the king's men
> Couldn't put Humpty Dumpty back together again
> *But Jesus showed up and put him back whole*
> *Then helped him rewrite what the enemy stole*

God always meets us where we are—but He doesn't leave us there.

"He brought me up also out of a horrible pit, out of the miry clay, and set my feet upon a rock, and established my goings." —Psalm 40:2

God loves you. He is there to help you. He knows right where you are at. He understands. And he will help you rewrite your story.

Let's talk about some ways that will help you change the default, uproot the strongholds, and rewrite that beautiful story:

1. Find and read the "In Him" Scriptures.

In order to rewrite your story, you have to know what to rewrite. The "In Him" scriptures paint the picture of who you really are in Christ. They have rewritten your story, portraying what Jesus did for you when you became a new creation in Christ. These scriptures are found in the epistles, from the book of Romans to 3 John in the New Testament.

Highlight every verse that says *in Him*, *in Whom*, or *in Christ*.

These verses reveal who you really are. Write them down. Speak them daily. Meditate on them. Let them become more real to you than anything your past has ever said.

Romans 12:2 says, "And be not conformed to this world: but be yet transformed by the renewing of your mind, that ye may prove what is that good, and acceptable, and perfect, will of God."

II Corinthians 10:4 says, "(For the weapons of our warfare are not carnal, but mighty through God to the pulling down of strongholds)."

Renewing your mind with the word of God changes false belief systems and pulls down strongholds. It will take some work on your end, but the payoff is life altering. It's freedom from shame, freedom from inferiority, freedom from debilitative thinking, freedom from a victim mentality.

Where you once believed you were bad or unworthy—marked by shame—these verses will reveal the truth: in Him, you are washed clean by His precious blood. You are righteous, not shameful. Forgiven, not condemned. Loved, not tolerated. Free, not bound.

If you once felt like a failure, unloved, not belonging or not worthy, you'll discover that God chose you before the foundation of the world. You are deeply loved, accepted in the Beloved, and created with divine purpose and potential. God doesn't see you as an outcast—He sees you as His own, full of promise and destiny. You are highly treasured and loved.

2. Pray the Ephesians prayers over yourself daily.

These powerful prayers are found in Ephesians 1:17–23 and 3:14–19. Put your name in them and speak them out loud—often. Daily. God's Word has the power to rewire your thinking and open your spiritual understanding.

These prayers are vital as you begin to discover who you are in Christ. At first, some In Him verses may feel unfamiliar or hard to grasp. That's okay. These prayers will illuminate the truth, helping the eyes of your understanding be enlightened.

Stay with it. Keep praying these prayers. As you do, your story will be rewritten—by the power of the Holy Spirit working through God's Word.

3. Meditate the Word.

You've found the scriptures. You're praying the Ephesians prayers. The next step is to meditate.

When you meditate on the Word, it begins to take root—it starts to transform your thinking from the inside out. Strongholds formed by past experiences and painful events begin to loosen. Meditation allows God's truth to go deep, uprooting lies that have kept you stuck or feeling small.

As you meditate on who you are in Christ, your old identity is replaced by the truth of your new one. When your thoughts change, your life changes.

Take one scripture a day. Think about it. Speak it quietly to yourself. Apply it to your life. For example, if you read, *"God so loved the world..."*—pause and say, "That means He loves me, because I'm part of that world." Then ask,

"What does it mean that God loves me? How does that affect how I see myself today? How does it impact this situation I'm facing?" This is meditation, thinking about the Word.

To rewrite your story from victim to victor, meditating on God's Word isn't optional—it's essential.

4. Change what you say.

Your words matter. If you want your story to change, your mouth has to agree with what God says about you.

You might get excited reading, *"I can do all things through Christ who strengthens me,"*—but if the moment you face a challenge you say, *"Oh, I could never do that. I'm not smart enough, good-looking enough, athletic enough…"*—then your story won't change. You're speaking the old script instead of the new one.

If you're going to start seeing yourself the way God sees you, your words must line up with His. We believe what we repeatedly say about ourselves—so pay attention to your words. Stop agreeing with fear, shame, and limitation.

Instead of saying, *"I'm not good enough,"* start saying what God says: *"I have the Greater One living on the inside of me and I can do all things through Christ."* Instead of saying, *"I'm too shy,"* start saying what God says: *"I am bold as a lion."* Instead of saying, *"No one likes me,"* start saying, *"God's favor surrounds me like a shield and I am accepted in the beloved."*

Your words don't just reflect your beliefs—they shape them. Speak the truth until it takes root. Your words are lifelines. They will renew your mind, stabilize your emotions, and empower you to live as the victor you already are in Christ.

The Ugly Duckling

Remember the story of *The Ugly Duckling*?

He looked nothing like the other ducks. From the beginning, he was different—and the rejection came quickly. Other animals teased him and pushed him aside. He didn't belong, even though he longed to. He wanted to spread his wings, to glide across the water like the other birds, but the taunts and shame held him back.

After a long, harsh winter spent hiding in a cave, he emerged—exhausted, hopeless, and ready to give up. But as he approached a pond and glanced into the water, something stopped him. His reflection had changed.

He wasn't the "ugly duckling" anymore. He had become a beautiful swan.

Just then, a group of swans—the most majestic of birds—saw him and welcomed him to join them. He had found his place.

It's a beloved story by Hans Christian Andersen, and so many of us relate to it more than we'd like to admit.

Maybe you feel like the ugly duckling—unwanted, overlooked, or out of place. But when you begin to rewrite your story with the truth of God's Word, everything changes.

You are not who you used to be. You are not what they said you were. You are not the sum of what you've been through.

You are blood-bought. You are loved. You are chosen. You are a victor—not a victim.

And one day, as you continue in the Word, you'll look into the reflection of truth and see it clearly:

You're no longer bound by past tragedies, circumstances, or rejection and shame. You are free. Free indeed.

Your story is not over. And the best part? You don't have to write it alone. God is the Author—and in His hands, your ending will be even more beautiful than you imagined.

Final Thoughts

You've got the victory. But now — it's time to believe who you are. You weren't created to live under the weight of defeat, fear, or insecurity. You were made to walk in the authority of the One who rescued you.

In the past people may have had control of what you thought of yourself, and how they shaped that story. But you have full control now, and only you can change that story. Your spouse, your parents, your best friend, not even your pastor can change your story. Only you. Through God and his Word. Through Him, you can do it.

Jesus didn't just save you — He **equipped** you. The old identity no longer defines you. The victim no longer gets to speak. The enemy no longer calls the shots. Your new identity shuts the door on the old one.

You are adopted. You are empowered. You are victorious. Your new story in Christ deserves to be written. Jesus died for that. Just for you.

You are Loved. God Loves You!

And once you begin to see that — everything begins to change. Strongholds of defeat, shame, and insecurity begin to lose their grip. They can't stay where truth has taken root.

You are not a victim — you are a victor. *But if you don't know that… you won't live that.*

In a crisis, our first instinct is often fear, passivity, or surrender. But here's the truth:

God has already made you victorious in Christ. You're not waiting for the victory — you're walking in it.

Still, you'll be vulnerable to the enemy's lies if you don't know who you are. And those lies? They'll talk you right out of your authority.

Jesus rescued you — but now you must rescue yourself into the truth. *You've been rescued and raised… don't lie down again.*

The enemy may have tried to write your story —but God already finished it in victory. When the enemy calls you a victim, remind him who's already won. Refuse the lie. Embrace the truth.

>You are not the victim. You are **Unshakeable**.

>God Loves *You…So Much!*

God Wants To Talk To *You*

To be Unshakeable, we must anchor ourselves in the voice of the One who knows all things.

You Were Born to Hear

Studies show that newborn babies can initially perceive around 800 different sounds. By six months, they start piecing together vowels. By nine months, they begin forming consonants. But how do they learn what any of it means?

They learn to recognize one voice—the one who holds, feeds, and loves them. That voice becomes an anchor, familiar in the midst of all the other noise.

Like that baby, you were born to hear your Father's voice.

When we're new to our walk with God, His voice can feel like just one sound in a sea of other noises—thoughts, emotions, fears, and people's opinions. Especially in moments of pressure, it can feel overwhelming to know what He's saying.

But here's the truth:

Yes, God speaks. Yes, you can hear Him. It's not spooky. It's not reserved for "special" people. And it's not through outside chaos—it's inward, quiet, and familiar. Just like a baby learns to recognize one voice, you will learn to recognize God's.

As we spend time with Him, the voice of God becomes familiar. It's not always loud, but it is always near—steady, present and faithful like a trusted friend.

God Speaks… Willingly

Before we discuss *how* God speaks, we need to remove the question of whether He will. Many people are uncertain about whether God wants to speak to them. Some think, *"God doesn't speak to me,"* or, *"If He does, it's only when He's mad or has something difficult to say,"* or *"Sometimes He will answer, but most of the time, He doesn't, you just never know."*

But nothing could be further from the truth.

From the beginning, God has been a communicator. In the garden, He walked and talked with Adam in the cool of the day. He spoke to Noah, Abraham, Moses, Samuel, and David. He guided His people through kings and prophets—and in the New Testament, He spoke to Jesus, Mary, Paul, Peter, and so many others.

He is not just the God of the Bible—He's the God of *right now*. He is still speaking. And not just to prophets or pastors. He speaks to *you* because He loves you, lives in you, and calls you, His child.

God's voice isn't something rare to stumble upon. It's something He *wants* you to hear.

"Call to Me and I will answer you and tell you great and unsearchable things you do not know." —Jeremiah 33:3

He is not hiding from you. He invites you into ongoing conversation—daily, personally, faithfully. And He speaks with the voice of a Father—sometimes firm, always loving, always good.

Sometimes, the biggest barrier to hearing God's voice is simply believing He actually *wants* to speak to us. If we think God is distant or silent, we may not lean in to listen.

But what if the issue isn't that He's not speaking—what if we just haven't learned to recognize His voice yet?

So, how does God speak?

Tuning Into The Right Voice

He speaks through peace. Through nudges. Through a knowing. Not usually through a megaphone—but through the still, small voice.

On June 18, 2023, the Titan Submersible tragically imploded while descending to view the Titanic wreckage. One of the passengers—a young man—had expressed deep hesitation about going. His mother later revealed that he didn't want to go but joined the trip to please his father.

Many people expect Him to speak through something dramatic—a dream, a booming voice, or a prophet with a loud word. And yes, He can speak that way. He has before, and He still does at times.

But that's not His usual way. If we expect the spectacular, we might miss the steady. God is Spirit—and His primary way of speaking is *Spirit to spirit.* That means it's inward. Personal. Gentle. Steady.

"For as many as are led by the Spirit of God, these are the children of God." (Romans 8:14)

Sometimes, we want signs. We want three confirmations, an open door, and maybe a cloud shaped like an arrow. But God doesn't need to send outward signs when He already lives inside us.

The Holy Spirit dwells within you and leads you from within—not through drama, but direction.

Once we understand that God truly wants to speak to us—and how He does—we can begin to recognize His voice with greater clarity. We'll explore that more in the next chapter. But for now, just remember this:

God is speaking. The question is, which voice are you tuning into?

An inward hesitation? It could be more than just nerves. It could be an inner warning—an inward sense.

We all face this: The inner voice of peace or caution…versus the outer voices of pressure, persuasion, or emotion.

God's voice won't always be the loudest, but it will be the most faithful.

This is why learning to recognize that inward voice is *essential*. When life is loud—when people are pushing, when fear is shouting, and when logic is arguing—you need to know which voice to trust.

You need to know the right voice.

And that voice—the voice of God—won't pressure or manipulate. It won't stir panic or confusion. It comes with peace, assurance, clarity, and wisdom, even when it challenges you or doesn't make perfect sense to your natural mind.

"But the wisdom that is from above is first pure, then peaceable, gentle, and easy to be intreated, full of mercy and good fruits, without partiality, and without hypocrisy." James 3:17

That's why training your heart to recognize His voice is vital. You don't want to wait until the storm hits to learn how to hear Him. You want to be familiar with His tone, pace, and peace so that when the pressure rises, you don't panic.

You *pause*. You *listen*. And you move with confidence because you know the One who's leading you.

You've learned the difference between the shouting of fear and the whisper of peace. You've practiced leaning into His presence. And now, when everything around you shakes—you don't.

To Be Unshakeable…Know Your Father Wants to Speak To You…Hear His Voice.

Let's bring it all together.

God wants to talk to you. God is talking to you.

You were born to hear Him. His voice is not far away. It's not for the elite or the ultra-spiritual. It's for you—His child.

He speaks willingly, leads gently, and speaks Spirit to spirit through peace, promptings, and the quiet assurance that rises from within.

You don't have to chase signs. You don't have to beg. You don't have to be perfect. You have to be willing to listen.

The more time you spend with Him, the more familiar His voice becomes. Like a baby turning her head to her mother's voice—you'll know when it's Him. Even in chaos. Especially in crisis.

Because when the storm is loud, the only voice that can steady you is His. And that's the voice you were created to follow.

And remember – God wants to talk to *You!*

When you believe the fact that God wants to speak to *you*, the more Unshakeable you'll become.

Hearing God in the Storm

Hearing is a beautiful gift. The sound of birds chirping in the morning, waves brushing the shore, or wind rustling through trees stirs our senses and settles our souls.

But there's a hearing even more precious—one that goes beyond the natural. It's the ability to hear the voice of the Holy Spirit.

Jesus said in *Matthew 11:15, "He that hath ears to hear, let him hear."* He wasn't just talking about physical ears. He invited us to intentionally lean in—to listen to His words and voice.

When life gets loud with bad news, fear, pressure, or confusion, and emotions are roaring, we must know how to hear the voice that matters most. What you hear in those moments matters deeply. *In Mark 4:24, Jesus again said, "Take heed what you hear."*

After receiving test results from the doctor that required more testing, I remember the option I had to call someone—family, friends, anyone who might offer some clarity. But instead of running to people, I ran to God. I asked the One who made my body what He had to say. As a result, peace flooded in—a peace that didn't come from answers but from His voice.

When we are the recipient of a bad report, we're tempted to gather opinions, to Google symptoms, to reach out for something that might calm us. But not every voice brings comfort. Some voices add weight, fear, and confusion.

That's why taking heed what you hear—especially in crisis—is a necessity. One unwise comment can pile more heaviness on an already difficult moment, even from someone close. What you hear either feeds your faith or fuels fear. Yes, we need to hear, but we need to hear the right words.

Power in God's Words

In the 1980s, the E.F. Hutton commercials had a simple message: "When E.F. Hutton talks, people listen." Why? Because he was seen as someone with authority and insight.

But what happens when the One who created the universe speaks?

Hebrews 11:3 says that the worlds were framed by the Word of God. When Jesus spoke to a fig tree, it withered. When He spoke to a storm, it ceased. When He spoke healing, it disarmed disease. His words change reality.

In times of crisis, that's the voice we need to hear. Not opinions. Not theories. Not even well-meaning advice. We need *God's Words* because they bring light, direction, peace, truth and most importantly, faith.

Faith comes by hearing and hearing by the Word of God. If we are in a situation where we need to know the escape route, or we need a miracle, we have to hear from God. If we don't hear from God, we can't base our faith on anything solid.

More than anything else we need in a crisis…is God's Word. Yes, He speaks through the written Word, but He also speaks to our spirits (which we'll talk about more in the next chapter).

Think about it: when we reach out to someone in the middle of a crisis, what are we looking for? *Words.* Words of comfort. Words of reassurance. When we're hit with bad news—about our health, our finances, or our future—we long to hear: *"It's going to be okay."* We want words from the doctor, the banker, the friend—someone telling us there's hope.

In the same way, when we tune our ears to hear *God's words,* everything changes. Hopelessness, helplessness, and sudden grief start to lift—not because the situation has changed, but because *we've heard from Him.*

The real issue in most storms isn't the storm itself—it's whether or not we've heard from God.

If someone asked me to list ten things to do in a crisis, here's what I'd say:

1. Hear from God.
2. Hear from God.
3. Hear from God.
4. 4–10? You guessed it. Hear from God.

Everything else can come *after* that. But first—we need to hear from Him.

I am often amazed at some things that people go through and they will spell out every detail into a prayer request, and so many times as they are talking, I am thinking, *have you asked God about it?*

It is so clear what to do when you just aren't sure or when faced with something bigger than you – hear from God.

One word from God can change everything. It can shift a diagnosis, silence fear, create life, dispel despair, and bring clarity to chaos. "One word from God can change your life."
– Gloria Copeland.

"If you can teach people to follow their spirits, you can help them in every arena of their life."– Kenneth Hagin

God has all the answers, every answer you will ever need. And the Holy Spirit is in your spirit to reveal and to show you things.

Hear from God.

When Again Comes - Inquire *Again*

Sometimes things happen in our lives... and then they happen *again*. The cancer comes back. You lose the job again. The heartbreak returns.

When we've had a victory in an area, it's natural to go back to what worked last time—confessions, scriptures, certain prayers. But what happens when it doesn't work the same way this time?

It comes back to this: Did we hear from God—again?

We can't rely on yesterday's manna. The situation may look the same, but that doesn't mean the answer is. We must *inquire of the Lord again*, and hear what He says *this time.* When we do, we can anchor our faith in His specific word for that moment. This principle is vital, no matter how familiar the storm may feel.

We see this in 1 Chronicles 14:10:

"And David inquired of God, saying, Shall I go up against the Philistines? And wilt thou deliver them into mine hand? And the Lord said unto him, Go up; for I will deliver them into thine hand." David defeated the Philistines.

But then... they came back. Again.

"Therefore David inquired again of God; and God said unto him, Go not up after them; turn away from them, and come upon them over against the mulberry trees." (v. 14)

Same enemy. Different strategy. David didn't assume. He didn't default to what worked last time.

He inquired *again*.

He was stronger than before. The enemy was weaker than before. But David still asked. And because he did, he *won*.

When you're faced with bad news **again**—the diagnosis, the loss, the heartbreak—don't automatically go into default mode. *Go to the Lord—**again.***

So many people repeat what worked before, and when it doesn't move the mountain, frustration builds. The problem isn't always the resistance.

Sometimes, it's the lack of a *fresh word*. **When again comes... inquire again.** God may give you a new strategy. A new route. A new answer.

Ask Him questions like:

- Why is this happening again?
- Do I have surgery again?
- Do I take another job offer?

Whatever the situation, hear from God. Let His Word direct you—not the familiarity of your last victory.

It is *imperative* that we hear from God—***continually***. Even if the storm is still raging on the outside, when you have a word from God, the storm is over on the *inside*. His Word is final. That's what we put our faith in—not what it looks like.

Hearing in Crisis

We've talked about the importance of inquiring again—even when the storm looks familiar. But what about the moments when the storm hits *suddenly*? The kind of moment where you don't have hours to fast, think, or figure it out? In those times, what you've developed in the quiet times becomes critical.

There's a true story of a minister walking through New York City on the morning of 9/11, heading to his office. Just before one of the planes hit the first tower, he suddenly heard the Lord say, *"Run!"*

He obeyed—immediately.

His quick response saved his life. Had he not heard the Lord in that moment, his story may not be heard today. Jesus said, *"My sheep hear My voice." (John 10:27)*. That promise doesn't disappear in crisis. If anything, crisis makes hearing His voice even more essential. But hearing in crisis starts with listening in the quiet. When we build daily awareness of His voice, we'll recognize it instantly when we need it most.

What Are You Not Hearing?

Sometimes people face a challenge and do *everything they know to do*—they stand on the Word, make their confessions, and hold firm in faith. Or maybe they get the victory… only to face the exact same battle all over again.

It begs the question:

What are you not hearing?

Have we actually gone to the Lord and asked Him for help? Some people who go through situations that seem to linger and get worse say that they are doing all the right things—and if you try to suggest anything, they'll say, *"Oh, I've done that. I already know that."* But here's what often gets left out in all the doing:

Asking God the right questions.

The Holy Spirit is our Helper. He's our Coach. He wants to see us win against the enemy *more than we do*. He is wisdom. He is all-knowing. And He is willing to speak.

Have you asked,
- "Is there a question I should be asking that I am not?"
- "Why isn't this working?"
- "What am I not seeing?"
- "What do You want me to know?"

If we're not hearing from the Holy Spirit, we're probably not hearing the right thing.

When I was younger, my uncle and I used to shoot basketball together. He taught me a simple trick—a tiny adjustment in how I placed my fingers on the ball. And it worked. To this day, I still use it. And without that one small tip? I probably wouldn't make a single shot.

Here's the thing: anyone can toss a ball and hit the rim. Some can even skim the basket—close enough to *almost* score. But it's the *precise placement* of the fingers that gets the ball in the basket—winning points, winning the game.

Sometimes we're doing all the right things. We're close. The victory seems almost there. But nothing's breaking through.

What's missing?

We're not hearing from Him. Go to the Holy Spirit.

Ask:
- "What do I need to do?"
- "Is there something I need to stop doing?"
- "Is there a small adjustment—something simple I'm overlooking?"

Maybe it's a tweak. Maybe it's timing. Maybe it's nothing at all—except *keep standing*. But if we continue moving without stopping to ask… we might keep hitting the rim instead of making the shot.

He Speaks in the Whisper

In 1 Kings 19, Elijah was desperate. Earthquakes, fire, and fierce winds surrounded him. But God wasn't in the noise.

Then came a whisper. That's where God was. And Elijah heard Him. We live in a noisy world—breaking news, loud opinions, endless notifications, swirling thoughts. But God's voice hasn't changed.

It's still gentle. Still steady. Still speaking. *Are we quiet enough to hear it?*

Training Our Ears

Romans 10:17 reminds us: *"Faith comes by hearing..."* Spiritual hearing isn't automatic—it's developed. Just like our physical ears can grow dull from constant noise, our spiritual ears can become dim when flooded with fear, distraction, or emotional static.

But we can train our hearing. We can sharpen our sensitivity. Because it's not about the storm—it's about our ability to hear *in* the storm. If you've ever thought, *"I can't hear God right now... not with all this going on,"*

In 1 Kings 19, Elijah was desperate. Earthquakes, fire, and fierce winds surrounded him—but God wasn't in the noise. Then came a whisper.

That's where God was. And Elijah heard Him. We live in a noisy world—breaking news, loud opinions, phone notifications, and swirling thoughts. But God's voice hasn't changed. It's still gentle. Still steady. Still speaking.

Are we quiet enough to hear it?

Conclusion
In the chaos of life, hearing God's voice is not a luxury—it's your lifeline. His words stabilize when everything else shakes. They bring light into darkness.

Peace into fear. Direction into confusion.

This isn't just about survival—it's about victory.

The God who framed the universe is speaking. The question isn't whether He's speaking. It's whether we're tuning in.

So, in the noise, pause. Lean in. Listen.

Why does hearing God's voice matter in a storm? Because everything else gets loud in a storm; because wrong voices can mislead you and because God's voice alone can bring strategy, peace and direction.

Because when God speaks—and you listen - you become Unshakeable.

How To Hear God in Everyday Life

We established in the last chapter that God wants to speak to us, understanding that hearing his voice is vital to our lives.

Those are powerful truths—but how exactly does God speak to our spirits? What should we be listening for? And where is our "spirit," anyway?

The first thing to establish is this: God speaks to our spirits, and we hear Him in our spirits. That's different from hearing God through natural means like outward signs or audible voices. God *can* speak that way, of course—but that's not His usual method.

Let's take a closer look at what our spirit is, where it "lives," and how God communicates with our spirit—so we can recognize when He's speaking and respond confidently.

Who Are We?

We are a spirit, we have a soul, and we live in a body. First and foremost, we are spiritual beings.

Genesis 1:27 says, *"So God created man in his own image, in the image of God created he him; male and female created he them."*

John 4:24 tells us, *"God is a spirit: and they that worship him must worship him in spirit and in truth."*

And 1 Thessalonians 5:23 says, *"And the very God of peace sanctify you wholly, and I pray God your whole spirit and soul and body be preserved blameless unto the coming of our Lord Jesus Christ."*

These verses show that God is a spirit, and He made us just like Him—a spirit.

This is a foundational truth because God, as a spirit, speaks to His children *through* their spirits.

Let's think about it this way—have you ever considered how fish communicate with each other?

If you wanted to talk to a dolphin or a whale, you couldn't just swim up and start a conversation. They don't use words like we do because they weren't created to communicate the same way humans do. They're a different species. If you asked a whale, "What do you like about living in the ocean?" you wouldn't get a verbal response—not because it has nothing to say, but because it doesn't speak your language. Fish and marine animals communicate through body language, chemical signals, color changes, and vibrations.

In the same manner, if a silver-colored fish suddenly turned bright orange to warn you about a predator nearby, you'd probably think, *Wow, that was amazing—they changed colors!* You'd miss the message completely.

Why? Because you're not a fish. You're not tuned to that kind of communication.

In the same way, God communicates with us *spirit to spirit*—because we are spirit beings, and *He is a Spirit*. If we try to hear Him only with our physical ears, or if we're always looking for external signs or dramatic moments, we will miss what He's saying.

Just like you wouldn't try barking at your dog to say, "I love you," and expect a heartfelt response, we can't expect to hear God clearly if we're tuned only to the physical world. He doesn't speak through emotion, reason, or logic first—He speaks to our spirit.

Animals communicate one way. Humans another. And God—He speaks from His Spirit to our spirit.

That's why it's essential to become familiar with how He communicates—not just *that* He speaks, but *how* He speaks—so you can confidently recognize His voice in everyday life.

Sometimes, He leads with a deep sense of peace. Other times, it's a gentle nudge, a strong inner knowing, or what is called the inward witness.

But no matter the method, the channel is the same: Spirit to spirit.

Where Is The Spirit That God Communicates To?

To better understand where our spirit is, let's start by clarifying where it is *not*: It's not our body. God does not speak through our bodies.

So if we get goosebumps on our arm and assume God is speaking—nope. That's not how it works. God speaks to your spirit. Not your physical body.

Both Peter and Paul describe the *hidden man of the heart*— that's our spirit. This "hidden man" refers to the part of us we can't see. Our spirit isn't located in a visible or physical place. We are spirit beings housed in a body. And the center of all communication with the Lord happens in that spiritual core—our spirit.

In 1 Peter 3:4 it says:
"But let it be the hidden man of the heart, in that which is not corruptible, even the ornament of a meek and quiet spirit, which is in the sight of God of great price."

Paul echoes this in 2 Corinthians 4:16:
"...Though our outward man perish, yet the inward man is renewed day by day."

This "inward man" is our spirit—the part of us that never dies.

Proverbs 20:27 tells us,
"The spirit of man is the candle of the Lord, searching all the inward parts of the belly."

The Young's Literal Translation says,
"...searching all the inward parts of the heart."

Physically, we can't locate our spirit the way we would a bone or organ. You can't point to your spirit on a medical chart. But Scripture gives us clues—it often refers to the "inward parts" or the "belly" as the place where we sense God's direction.

This is what many call the "heart." Not the physical heart beating in your chest, but your spiritual heart—the core of your being. The real you.

Think about when someone says, *"Listen to your heart."* We know they're not talking about their physical organ shouting out instructions. They really mean, *"Follow what you know deep down on the inside. Trust what you sense in your spirit."*

Jesus referred to this in Mark 11:23:

"For verily I say unto you, That whosoever shall say unto this mountain, Be thou removed, and be thou cast into the sea; and shall not doubt in his heart, but shall believe that those things which he saith shall come to pass; he shall have whatsoever he saith."

That inner knowing, that inward witness, flows from your spirit. Romans 10:10 says, *"For with the heart man believes..."* That's not a physical process—it's spiritual. You believe, trust, and connect with God from your spirit, not your mind or emotions.

And Romans 10:8–10 says:

"But what saith it? The Word is nigh thee, even in thy mouth, and in thy heart: that is, the Word of faith, which we preach; that if thou shalt confess with thy mouth the Lord Jesus, and shalt believe in thine heart that God hath raised Him from the dead, thou shalt be saved. For with the heart man believeth unto righteousness; and with the mouth confession is made unto salvation."

So, where is your spirit? It's not floating around or hiding in your brain. The inner you—your spirit man, your inner person, the real you—lives in your body but functions in the spirit realm. We are a spirit. We have a soul. We live in a body.

We'll unpack this more as we explore how God communicates through your spirit into your spirit.

The Inward Witness

This is the number one way God will lead us. Some call it intuition, but it's deeper than that—it's a *knowing*. You don't know how you know—you *know*. You don't know why, but it's there—an undeniable awareness in your spirit.

Have you ever had a moment where something just rose up inside you, and you *knew* it—without anyone saying a word or lacking physical evidence? Maybe your daughter or a friend was pregnant, but she hadn't said anything. A quiet thought surfaced over lunch during the everyday conversation: *She's pregnant.* You didn't see anything. You didn't hear anything. But something inside you knew. And later—it turned out to be true.

You know, that you know.

Years ago, I entered a season of treatment at the City of Faith Hospital in Tulsa, Oklahoma—a facility with a special unit dedicated to helping those facing eating disorders and related challenges. After several months of intensive care, I was discharged. But the journey toward full healing was far from over. Deep down, I knew I needed to continue with the same doctor who had guided so much of my early progress. Starting over with someone new felt not only daunting but potentially disruptive. So, despite the fact that I now lived in another state, I made a firm decision to stay the course.

Determined not to lose momentum, I flew from my home state to Tulsa each week—just to see that one doctor. Many times, during those sessions, specific questions would rise to the surface—uncertainties about what might be or might not be. I'd raise the question, and once he gave his answer, I would often keep pressing, wanting clarity. At some point in those conversations, he would look me in the eye and calmly say, "I just know." I'd challenge him— "But how do you know?"—and without any tension, he would simply repeat, "I just know."

And the amazing part? He always *did* know. What he discerned would prove to be right every single time. He couldn't explain it in natural terms—he just had a knowing in his spirit. And that knowing led him.

That's how the inward witness works.

You'll have a strong sense in your spirit of something God is showing you. It may not make sense, but no one can talk you out of it. You just *know*.

After graduating high school in Honolulu, Hawaii, the Lord spoke to me about going to a particular bible school in Tulsa, Oklahoma. I don't mean an audible voice when I say He spoke, but hearing Him in my spirit. At the time, I knew nothing about this school, only the founder of the school.

A few days later, a magazine from that very ministry showed up in the mail. I instantly recognized what it was—and I was more than excited! Over the next nine months, I began preparing for the move from Hawaii to Tulsa. And even when voices or circumstances came up that seemed to contradict that decision, nothing could shake what I knew inside. I *knew* that I knew. Sure, there were last-minute jitters—but thanks to good, godly counsel from my pastor, I recognized them for what they were: jitters!

This knowing can't be duplicated in the natural realm. It's not based on logic or emotion. It's a spiritual knowing—an assurance and confidence that surpasses all understanding. It's the inward witness of the Holy Spirit.

Peace

In my own life, this has been one of the primary ways the Lord speaks to me—in my spirit—through peace. Not an outward feeling of happiness or calm, but a deep, inner peace that flows from the inside.

Colossians 3:15 (AMPC) says:
"And let the peace (soul harmony which comes) from Christ rule (act as umpire continually) in your hearts [deciding and settling with finality all questions that arise in your minds, in that peaceful state] to which as [members of Christ's] one body you were also called [to live]. And be thankful (appreciative) [giving thanks to God always]."

One year, while working as a hotel General Manager, I took a much-needed vacation. I didn't have any special plans—just a staycation to rest and recharge. One morning, I went out for coffee and had planned afterwards to drive to Mystic, Connecticut, to do a little shopping and have a quiet meal by the ocean. It was a perfect day for some peaceful R&R.

But pulling out of the coffee shop, I was suddenly overcome with an unusual peace about returning home. There was no logical reason for it. I had the whole day ahead of me. Still, I couldn't shake the sense that I was supposed to return home and spend the afternoon reading or napping.

I even questioned it: *"Why do I feel such a draw to do this—especially when I've been longing for the peace of the ocean?"*

Yet the peace rising from the inside was unmistakable. So, I followed it.

I went home. I read a little, then laid down and took a nap. Not long after, my phone dinged. It was a message from a friend informing me that a business friend of ours had been the victim of a shooting the night before. He had been life-flighted to a hospital—right in my area. From what I was told and knowing where he had been shot, it didn't sound like he had much time left. His eternity was hanging in the balance.

I immediately got in my car and drove to the hospital. He was in critical condition. But by God's grace, I was able to sit quietly with him. I had the chance to share the gospel in those last precious hours—or maybe days—of his life. Later, I went to see my manager, who knew him as well, and a few of us went back to the hospital to say private goodbyes.

A day or so later, he passed away.

If I had ignored that gentle, peaceful nudge and gone out of town as planned, I would've missed the opportunity to be alone with him—to speak eternal words at an eternal moment. God knew the text message would come that afternoon, and He lovingly directed me to be in place and nearby so, just in time, I could go and visit before our friend passed away.

Look inside to hear from the Lord in times of crisis or in simple, quiet moments. One of the primary ways He speaks is through peace. It's often a gentle, inward flow pulling you in a particular direction or toward (or away from) something. Once you experience that leading, you'll begin to recognize it more and more.

If we make it a habit to turn inward and follow peace in our everyday dealings, we'll learn to discern it clearly when the stakes are high.

When I say turn inward or look inside it means get quiet of all the outside noise and thoughts and just listen to what you sense in your spirit. Where is the peace? What are you sensing inside? Remember, the Spirit is always speaking…learn to turn your spiritual ears, so to speak, to hear his voice or leadings in peace.

At times, the peace may not make sense to your mind. It may even seem odd, like it did for me that day. But if we're going to grow in hearing His leadings, we must learn to follow peace, even when we don't fully understand it.

Sometimes, God's leading shows up in small things. You might feel a sudden peace about taking a different route to work or school—and only later discover there was an accident on your usual path. Or you're standing in the grocery store, thinking, "I really should start eating healthier." You reach for a particular healthy item, but something inside just doesn't sit right. It's not fear or anxiety—just a quiet, unsettled feeling. A pause. A red light. A lack of peace.

I've ignored that before. I brought the item home, tucked it away in the pantry, and never touched it. Weeks later, I'd end up tossing it in the trash, thinking, "I knew I shouldn't have bought that."

Sometimes, the Lord uses the smallest moments to teach us to follow His peace. If we can recognize it in the grocery aisle, we'll be more confident recognizing it in life-altering decisions. Oftentimes an opportunity will come our way and we may have a real peace about it…or not…this is Him leading you. No matter how good the opportunity looks, if there is no peace, a lack thereof, don't do it. Follow peace.

Peace may not seem significant at the time, but it's part of learning how the Lord leads. When we pause and check for peace—even in the small things—we're exercising our spiritual sensitivity. We're training ourselves to listen.

And here's something else I've learned: when the peace comes, don't try to interpret it.

I once felt a deep peace about a situation and assumed it meant everything would turn out a certain way. I was wrong. It *did* work out—but not in the way I expected. God's peace doesn't always mean the outcome will match our interpretation. It simply means He's in it. He's guiding. And He's asking us to trust without needing all the details.

That's the nature of peace-led guidance—it often doesn't explain itself in advance. It doesn't always come with a reason or a roadmap. But when you learn to trust that inner peace, you begin to walk in step with the Spirit.

We read before *Colossians 3:15, "Let the peace of Christ rule in your hearts..."* The word "rule" carries the idea of an umpire calling the shots in a game—making decisions when things are uncertain or disputed. In other words, peace is meant to be the deciding factor.

So let it rule. Let it overrule your anxious thoughts. Let it guide your next steps. Let it settle your soul when logic screams and emotions flare. The more you practice turning inward and recognizing peace in your everyday life, the more prepared you'll be when the larger challenges come.

You won't have to guess or wrestle. You'll know.

God's peace doesn't shout. It doesn't force. It gently leads. And when it comes, follow it. Trust it. Honor it. Because more often than not, that quiet leading sets you up for something you couldn't see coming—but He could.

And He always leads in peace.

The Still Small Voice

1 Kings 19:12 (NLT)
"And after the earthquake there was a fire; but the Lord was not in the fire. And after the fire, there was the sound of a gentle whisper."

I still remember that day in prayer, on my knees, face to the floor. About nine months earlier, we'd lost a family member, and now we had just received devastating news—a close relative had been diagnosed with a severe form of cancer.

It was one of those moments when you know you need to hear from God. No fluff. No guessing. It's just a real word to hold onto.

As I prayed, seeking the Lord with my whole heart, I heard it—the still, small voice. It wasn't audible, but it was clear. Deep in my spirit, I heard the Lord say, *"It's going to be okay."*

That still small voice became my anchor. Through the journey that followed—the uncertainty, the doctor reports, the symptoms increasing and decreasing—I clung to that word. I claimed it as mine, reminded God of it, and even reminded the enemy of it when doubt tried to creep in. That morning, on the floor, God had spoken—and as always, His word held. That family member came out in victory.

Elijah, too, knew what it was like to hear a quiet word that changed everything...Elijah knew something about the still, small voice, too. After a powerful showdown on Mount Carmel, where he witnessed fire fall from heaven, he ran for his life—discouraged and afraid. Alone in a cave, he was visited by an angel who gave him food, rest, and direction. Then God called him to stand on the mountain.

There, Elijah experienced dramatic events—wind, an earthquake, and fire—but Scripture carefully tells us that *God was not in any of those things.*

Then came a gentle whisper. That still small voice.

That's where God was.

I can't stress enough how important it is to get *God's word* on a matter—especially when it involves someone else's life, health, or future. That whispered word in prayer, that still small voice in your spirit, becomes an anchor in the storm. It's not just a moment of comfort; it becomes a sword in your hand.

This is why we must learn to hear God in our spirits. His voice won't always shout above the noise. But when we practice listening, slow down, and tune in, we begin to recognize His leading. And when a crisis hits, we won't be scrambling to figure out if it's Him. We'll already know.

Sometimes, it is just a whisper.

Not something you hear with your natural ears, but with the ears of your heart—your spirit.

How Do I Know It's Not Just Me?

This question is one of the biggest hindrances to people developing sensitivity in hearing God's voice:

"What if it's just me thinking this? What if it's not God?"

It's a common concern—and a valid one. But the truth is: you're going to miss it sometimes. We all do.

Have you ever turned to someone and asked, "Did you call my name?" Only for them to say, "No."

You could've sworn you heard it. But no one did—or at least, not the person you thought.

Or maybe when your child was a baby, you thought you heard them cry, only to check and find them sound asleep. Yet after days and weeks of caring for that baby, you became so familiar with their voice that you could pick it out in a crowded room, even above other children. You just *knew* it was them.

It's the same with God.

The more time you spend with Him, the more familiar His voice becomes. The more you respond to His leadings—even the small ones—the more you'll begin to distinguish between your own thoughts and His promptings. Just like a musician becomes familiar with the sound of each note, or a child recognizes the voice of their parent in a crowd, we grow in spiritual sensitivity through intentional practice.

Hearing from God isn't a mystical talent reserved for a few—it's a daily relationship we can all develop. The more we walk with Him, the more tuned in we become. And soon, we stop second-guessing. Instead of asking, "Was that just me?" we begin to trust, "That was Him." His voice becomes a part of us—woven into the rhythm of our lives.

It takes time. It takes practice. But most of all, it takes a relationship.

Can I Hear Him in a Crisis?

You may have heard stories of people who felt a prompting from God in a life-or-death moment, and you've wondered: *Would I have heard that too?*

There's a story of a preacher who had traveled overseas to minister. When he arrived by train—during a time when that country had groups that were hostile toward certain types of people—the local pastor who was supposed to pick him up had the wrong day marked on his calendar. There was no one to pick him up from the train.

Unfortunately, this wasn't just a scheduling mix-up—it was dangerous. A violent group that often targeted people like him—outsiders who matched a particular profile—began to encircle him, and this minister found himself alone, unguarded, and suddenly surrounded by nearly forty hostile men, known for killing those who entered their territory.

In that split second, God spoke.

"Spin like a top!" The preacher didn't question it. He obeyed. Right there on the train platform, he began to spin. Then the Lord said, "Curse them!" It sounded bizarre—but again, he obeyed. When he stopped spinning, something miraculous had happened. When he stopped spinning, every person in that mob was frozen—unable to move. The Lord said, "Run!" and as the minister ran, his help showed up at just the right time. He was safe.

It's a wild story. But it begs the question—would I have heard God in that kind of situation?

That's a fair question. And the answer often comes down to this:

Have I trained my ears to hear Him in the quiet, everyday moments?

Because the truth is, you *can* hear God in a crisis. But learning to recognize His voice doesn't begin in the middle of the storm—it starts long before.

It's often hard to hear anything clearly during trauma or bad news. That's why practicing daily—when things are calm—prepares us for those moments.

Like the mother with her child, you begin to recognize the sound of His whisper because you've spent time together. Daily time in the Word, time praying in the Spirit, and quiet moments just sitting and listening—these are the things that develop our spiritual ears.

You might say, *"But I don't hear Him."*

Don't worry—you will. You'll come to know His voice. You'll recognize His peace, His whisper, His promptings. But it takes time. Intentional time spent sitting with Him, getting familiar with how He speaks. Leaning in to hear Him in the quiet moments of everyday life—through the inward witness, the peace, and the still small voice.

Make it a goal to become more familiar with how God speaks to you each day. Journal the leadings. Write down the nudges, the whispers, the moments of peace. Track what worked and what didn't. As you do, you'll become more attuned to His voice.

My dad used to have me pray every night before bed and then have me listen quietly for what God might be saying to me. I'd write it down in my journal. The next day, he'd ask, "What did God say to you last night?" And I would read aloud whatever I felt the Lord had spoken. Sometimes, I didn't hear anything at all. But over time, with practice and consistency, I started to recognize when He was speaking— and how He speaks. It was a habit that taught me to learn to listen— *thank you, Dad.*

Apart from listening with our ears, watching what we say is vitally important. Instead of saying things like, *"I wish I could hear God speak to me like He talks to Minister So and So,"* or *"I don't know what God is saying to me or if He is even speaking at all,"* start agreeing with what the Word says, and confess that you are His sheep and you hear His voice and the voice of a stranger you will not follow. This is very important for if we continually disagree with the truth of God's words with our mouth, we will convince ourselves of a disbelief and it will hinder us hearing from God.

Jesus said in John 10:3-5
3 To him the porter openeth; and the sheep hear his voice: and he calleth his own sheep by name, and leadeth them out.
4 And when he putteth forth his own sheep, he goeth before them, and the sheep follow him: for they know his voice.
5 And a stranger will they not follow, but will flee from him: for they know not the voice of strangers.

You are His sheep! You can hear His voice and the voice of a stranger you will not follow! That's great news! You can hear your Father!

But we have a part to play. If we don't make a concerted effort to learn His voice daily, it will never progress. God wants to speak to us daily, all throughout the day, in every situation. He wants to laugh with us, walk with us and talk with us moment by moment.

If we want to be Unshakeable in times of crisis, we have to be people who know how to hear God's voice. This is not an option; it's a downright necessity.

But it doesn't begin in the storm.

It begins in the quiet, ordinary moments—when we tune our hearts to hear the One who speaks Spirit to spirit.

And when we do, we become people who are not shaken because we have heard from God and no words are more powerful and sure than God's words during a storm.

God is always speaking—are we listening? Listen and be Unshakeable!

Shut Thy Mouth ... And Open It

On October 7, 2023, a tragic event unfolded as individuals were captured and taken hostage by Hamas. Every released hostage carries a unique story of survival that shapes their life and our understanding of resilience. One remarkable tale stands out in this chapter, highlighting the incredible strength and influence of words. It's a testament to the profound impact of the words that are spoken.

A young woman, after being released from captivity, joyfully told her father repeatedly how she had managed to escape *alive*. It was clear that she had survived, but her repetitive statement hinted at a deeper story behind her experience. Their story reflected the biblical truth that our words possess immense power to create, destroy, and declare life or death.

Later, we learned that the story was what her father continued to say day after day, that '*his daughter would come home, alive.*'

Proverbs 18:20 states, "Death and life are in the power of the tongue: and they that love it shall eat the fruit thereof."

The power of words to bring life into a crisis.

This is the power of speaking faith-filled words — they aren't empty statements but declarations of God's words that can pierce through the darkest circumstances. When extenuating circumstances all around you try to silence your faith, your words become a weapon, pushing back against fear, doubt, and despair.

Results From The Father's Words

In the midst of a major crisis, what we say—or don't say—matters greatly. Our words are like the rudder of a ship, steering us either out of the storm or deeper into it.

Consider the father whose daughter had been missing for over a year. Imagine the pressure he faced—anxiety and grief knocking constantly at the door of his mind. Thoughts of her never returning, fears of her condition, and the unknown must have overwhelmed him. Yet, despite the emotional turmoil, he refused to allow fear to dictate what he would say. Instead, he chose to speak life into what seemed like a dead situation.

Prov 4:22 "For they (God's Words) are life unto those that find them, and health to all their flesh."

That choice wasn't easy. Every day, he had to push back the fearful thoughts and resist the temptation to speak words of hopelessness. Silence can be powerful, too, in moments like that. Sometimes, the best thing you can do is hold your tongue until you're ready to speak words of faith and truth.

When it feels like there's no way out, your back is against the wall, or fear insists there's no hope, remember this: You have control. Even when everything seems impossible, you can guard your mouth and speak words that align with God's truth. And in those moments when you don't know what to say—don't rush to speak. Let your silence become a moment of strength rather than weakness.

Our Words are Weapons

In every battle, God provides an arsenal of powerful weapons to use against the enemy—and one of the most powerful is our words. We see this clearly in David's life when he faced the giant Goliath.

Like many of us, David found himself facing a crisis far greater than his resources, strength, or understanding. From a natural standpoint, David's chances seemed hopeless. Goliath was massive—his size alone was intimidating. In addition to Goliath's advanced weaponry and experience as a warrior, it seemed David didn't stand a chance.

But Goliath just didn't have strength; his words were weapons. He spewed out threats so powerful that all of Israel trembled with fear. Goliath's words were designed to predict David's defeat before the battle even began. His bellowing threats were sent to unsettle David with fear-filled words that would shape David's thinking—and, ultimately, his outcome.

No matter how threatening Goliath's words and influences were, God's words when spoken in faith were more powerful.

David didn't let Goliath's words have the final say. He fired back with words of his own—words of covenant, confidence, and victory. David had already declared his win before he ever released a stone from his sling. And just as David spoke, it happened. The words he declared became a reality, securing his own and Israel's future.

Like David, we all face words that try to intimidate—frightening doctor's reports, financial threats, or fears of loss. In those moments, it's tempting to speak what we see or feel—to give voice to doubt, despair, or destruction. To agree with the enemy. To agree with Goliath. But that's when we must be careful. Instead of agreeing with the situation, we must speak words that agree with God's truth.

We don't deny the reality—we deny its power to define our outcome. David didn't agree with Goliath's words because they weren't the truth. No matter what the situation looks like—or what it's saying to you—remember: facts are real, but God's Word is truth.

Yes, it was a fact that Goliath was massive, strong, and skilled in battle. But the truth? David had a covenant with God. And God is more powerful than any enemy—and faithful to stand behind His promise.

That same truth still shatters the enemy's plans today. A bad report may be factual—but God's Word is truth. Jesus said in *John 8:32, "And you shall know the truth, and the truth shall make you free."* He didn't say, *"You shall know the facts, and the facts will make you free."* No—it's truth. And truth, spoken, sets things into motion.

A preacher told a story about a woman and her four children who were driving down the road when they were involved in a terrible car accident. The children survived, but the mother was killed instantly upon impact. After stabilizing the children, authorities placed the woman's body in a bag and transported her to the morgue.

When they called the woman's mother to notify her of the death, her response was this: "Oh, all she needs is resurrection power. That's all she needs!"

She refused to let her words agree with death. Although she lived in another state, she immediately made plans to come—and spent the entire day and a half journey praying in the Spirit.

Back at the morgue, something remarkable happened. The lifeless body began to show signs of life. Long story short, the woman came back to life and was quickly transferred to the hospital. When her mother arrived, she continued to speak life over her daughter.

Over the next several months, that daughter made a full recovery. It took time, but the mother never stopped speaking God's Word and declaring life.

She was not intimidated by the report. She refused to agree with the tragedy. Her resolve was simple: to speak life into the situation—and that's exactly what happened. God's Word carries life-giving, circumstance-changing, creative power.

The problem is rarely the situation itself. More often, the problem is the words we speak in response—especially when they are not words of the Word

Words have power—far more than we often realize. Your words can shape your outcome, whether you are facing a health crisis, financial struggle, or personal heartbreak. Like David, speak words of life, victory, and hope.

Romans 4:17
"...and calleth those things that be not as though they were."

This is how God operates. He doesn't speak based on what is—He speaks based on what *will be.* He calls things that don't exist yet as if they already do. That's how creation happened. That's how covenant works. And as His children, we are called to imitate Him.

God didn't look into the darkness and say, "Wow, it's really dark."

He said, "Let there be light."

He didn't deny the reality—He just spoke a higher truth into it. And when we speak in alignment with His Word, we do the same. We don't call it as we see it—we call it as **He** says it.

Words spoken have tremendous power to effect change. Speak God's words.

It Starts in the Day to Day

If controlling your words feels overwhelming — especially in times of trouble — it may be a sign that this discipline is missing in your daily life: the discipline of intentionally training your mouth to agree with God's Word.

Like many principles discussed in this book, the key to remaining firm and *Unshakeable* when life feels like an earthquake is building strong habits *before* the crisis. The time to learn how to guard your words isn't in the heat of the moment — it's in the quiet, everyday moments when things seem ordinary.

God's principles aren't just designed for life's major storms—they're intended to guide us in daily life. It's in the routine frustrations—the flat tire, the unexpected bill, the unexpected computer crash before a deadline—that we train ourselves to respond with words of victory-minded words instead of words of frustration or defeat.

If we allow God's Word to shape our responses to those smaller pressures, we'll be prepared to respond in faith when more significant challenges arise. Just like an athlete trains, long before stepping into the competition, developing the proper habits now will make the correct response automatic when the pressure is on.

Consider it like muscle memory — the more consistently you practice speaking life, the more natural it becomes. So, when that unexpected bad report comes, or fear knocks at your door, your trained response will be to speak words of faith, life, and victory — because it's what you've been practicing all along.

The battle isn't just won in the crisis; it's prepared for in the daily.

What You Say Every Day

Guarding our mouths isn't just about avoiding lies, curse words, or crude jokes—although that's certainly part of it. Often, the most damaging words are the casual, thoughtless expressions we pick up from friends, family, or coworkers—phrases that may seem harmless but actually undermine our faith and confuse our spirits.

Words like:

- "I'm never going to get ahead."
- "This always happens to me."
- "I just can't catch a break."
- "Oh, that just scared me to death!"
- "I can't afford that!"
- "I thought I was going to die laughing!"
- "Well, it's flu season again! Every year, I come down with it."

- "We all have to die of something someday!"
- "Well, when one thing breaks, everything breaks—it happens all the time!"

These statements may seem small, but they carry weight. Words create pathways in our thinking, and when we repeatedly speak words that contradict God's promises—even jokingly—we train ourselves to expect defeat and we start to believe what we say.

The enemy knows the power of words. He's aware that if he can condition us to speak negative phrases casually — when we aren't thinking — then those exact destructive words will come out of our mouths when pressure hits. Why? Because we've unknowingly trained ourselves to default to those words.

In moments of crisis, we often reach for what's familiar. If we've spent months or years casually saying things like, "That just makes me sick!" or "I'm just sick and tired of such and such!" then when a genuine challenge arises—like a bad doctor's report or unexpected financial trouble—those same fearful words will be our instinctive response.

But when we train ourselves to speak words of faith in our everyday lives, those life-giving words will be the first thing that rises in times of trouble. Instead of declaring defeat, we'll declare what God has promised:

- "No weapon formed against me will prosper!"
- "By His stripes, I am healed."
- "I have never seen the righteous forsaken!"

The tongue is a powerful tool, but if we've been using it casually or carelessly, it won't work *for* us when we need it most — instead, it will work *against* us.

We must believe that words are not just sounds—they are seeds, tools, and *weapons*. If we don't believe this, we won't treat our words with the carefulness we need to walk in victory.

In a moment of crisis, we need a strong spirit consistently nourished with the Word of God. That strength is shaped by the words we speak every day.

Your words are building something — make sure they're building the right things.

Conclusion

Throughout this chapter, we've explored the incredible power of our tongue — a power that can shape circumstances, bring life or death, and determine the outcome of situations we face. I pray this has deepened your understanding of the significance of your words.

If we commit to watching our words daily — pausing before we speak, identifying phrases we've carelessly adopted from the world, and refusing to repeat them — we will begin building new habits. Those habits will strengthen our faith and reinforce the results of speaking God's Word in every situation.

When a bad report comes — and they inevitably will — we won't make things worse by speaking fear or defeat. Instead, we'll be prepared to respond with faith-filled words that create a pathway for victory. Our words won't give the enemy an open door to bring further destruction — they'll shut him out and invite God's power in.

If you want to live *Unshakeable*, guarding your tongue is not optional — it's essential.

Victory isn't just about what you believe but what you boldly declare.

Your words build your life—or break your hedge. So, speak like someone who's born to win.

        Stay Unshakeable…Watch Thy Mouth

The Setup

In the early 1980s, a man's world turned upside down. One day, he was a successful businessman. The next, he was fighting to salvage his reputation. His timeshare company had merged with another firm in Honolulu—a move that seemed smart at the time. But what followed was a nightmare.

Almost overnight, he found himself buried in legal battles, with the FBI, IRS, and FTC launching investigations over a crime that never happened. It was a calculated setup—carefully designed to ruin him.

For over a decade, his family lived under the weight of that lie. Sleepless nights. Endless questions. Fear of what might come next. Looking back, it's clear how deliberately the trap had been laid. One wrong partnership spiraled into a web of false accusations and ceaseless scrutiny. It wasn't just unfair—it was intentional.

That story hits close to home. Closer than most would ever guess.

But the attack failed.

Welcome to *The Setup*—where things aren't always as they seem.

When you're hit with bad news, the enemy hopes you'll focus only on the surface — the problem, the pain, the panic. He doesn't want you to pause and ask, *What's really going on here?* But when you do, something shifts. You start to see with spiritual eyes. You realize this isn't just an attack — it's a setup.

And not just any setup — a trap, carefully baited to pull you out of faith and into fear.

But you don't have to take the bait.

The Anatomy of a Setup

Every trap has components: bait, timing, and placement. The bait draws you in — it might be fear, offense, discouragement, or pressure. The timing is strategic — often right after a victory, or in a moment of vulnerability. And the placement? It's hidden in plain sight.

If you've ever wondered why something hit you "out of nowhere," you're not alone. But the truth is, these setups rarely come from nowhere. They're often the result of long-laid plans the enemy hopes you never notice.

In the above case, the bait was a business opportunity. The timing? Just after a period of success. The placement? A partnership that looked like progress but was really poison.

And that's how the enemy works. He doesn't need to show up in a red suit with a pitchfork. All he needs is a well-timed lie wrapped in something that looks good.

But when you understand the anatomy of a setup, you start asking better questions: *Who's really behind this? What is the purpose? What is their strategy?*

Those questions can save your life.

Recognizing Satan's Deception

Satan's setups almost always begin with deception. He's not just a liar — he's called the father of lies.

John 8:44 says:

44 You are of your father the devil, and the lusts of your father yet will do. He was a murderer from the beginning, and abode not in the truth, because there is no truth in him. When he speaketh a lie, he speaketh of his own: for he is a liar, and the father of it.

He uses half-truths, twisted facts, and emotional manipulation to draw people into spiritual traps.

He did it with Eve: *Did God really say...?*
He did it with Jesus: *If You are the Son of God...*
He does it with us: *If God really loved you, why would this be happening?*

The deception always questions God's word, your identity, or His goodness. If the enemy can distort what you believe, he can control how you respond.

But when you can identify the deception early, you can cut it off before it sets its hooks.

Seeing Through the Setup

I remember the moment I first flew home after my dad received his diagnosis. It was the kind of news that could rock anyone — the kind that makes your heart drop. But strangely, I wasn't shaken. I didn't zero in on the diagnosis itself. It wasn't that it was ignored — bur knowing there was something else going on. I could see it so clearly: this was a setup from the enemy, a desperate attempt to derail what God was doing in my dad's life.

I found myself almost *shaking my head in disbelief* as I sat with my parents. "Don't you see what's happening here?" I said. "This isn't just about a diagnosis. The enemy is trying to hijack God's plan — but he's not going to succeed."

In that moment, knowledge gave me peace. Clarity replaced fear. It broadened the scope of what only the enemy wanted us to see.

When you can spot the setup, you stop panicking. You stop giving the problem all the power. You remember who you are, and who your God is. That changes everything.

Knowledge Shields You From Harm

Proverbs 11:9 says, *"Through knowledge the righteous are delivered."*

It's not enough to just feel your way through crisis. You need discernment. Spiritual intelligence. The ability to see the setup for what it is — and choose a different response.

That's why staying close to God's Word is so vital. It sharpens your spiritual senses and keeps your heart anchored in truth when the storm hits.

In a setup, ignorance is costly. But knowledge is a shield.

Cutting Through the Enemy's Lies

The enemy doesn't come with a label. His traps are wrapped in logic, coated in emotion, and delivered in moments when you feel most vulnerable. That's why his lies can sound so believable.

"You'll never be the same."

"Your life is ruined."
"God must be punishing you."
"If you were stronger, this wouldn't be happening."

When those lies swirl, it's easy to sink into hopelessness. But here's the key: just because the thought comes, doesn't mean you have to keep it.

God's Word is your lie detector.

When Jesus was tempted in the wilderness, He didn't argue with Satan or get emotional. He responded with, *"It is written."* Truth cut through the lies every time. That's your strategy, too. When the trap is baited with fear, anxiety, or self-doubt, you fight back with what's true.

You don't need more opinions. You need truth.

Jesus's Strategy: Outwitting the Setup

One of the best biblical examples of someone who *saw through the setup* was Jesus.

In John 8 we find the story of the woman caught in the act of adultery.

John 8:3-7

3 And the scribes and Pharisees brought unto him a woman taken in adultery; and when they had set her in the midst,
4 They say unto him, Master, this woman was taken in adultery, in the very act.
5 Now Moses in the law commanded us, that such should be stoned: but what sayest thou?

6 This they said, tempting him, that they might have to accuse him. But Jesus stopped down, and with his finger wrote on the ground, as though he heard them not.
7 So when they continued asking him, he lifted up himself, and said unto them, He that is without sin among you, let him cast a stone at her.

The Pharisees were trying to brand Jesus as a false teacher and to do that, they needed to trap Him. They were referring to the Mosaic law in Deuteronomy 22:22-24. If Jesus had said no to stoning the woman, he would break the Jewish law. But if He had said yes to stoning her, He would've violated Roman law, which forbade Jews from carrying out capital punishment.

It was a setup—plain and simple.

But Jesus saw right through it. Instead of answering their trap, He stooped down and began writing in the sand. They continued to pressure him for an answer. Jesus remained unshaken. He didn't react to pressure-He responded with wisdom. Instead, he told them in *v. 7 "....He that is without sin among you, let him first cast a stone at her."*

The set up? Averted. Completely.

This wasn't the only time the Pharisees and Sadducees tried to trap Him. They asked about paying taxes to Caesar (Matthew 22:17), about the resurrection (Matthew 22:23), and which commandment was the greatest (Matthew 22:36).

Jesus avoided every trap that the enemy had set for Him. He knew something far above their schemes to trap Him – He knew God's Word.

Embracing the Power of Truth

There's something liberating about truth. Even when it's hard, truth clears the fog and gives you footing. When you understand that not every storm is random—and that some situations are setups—you begin to move with wisdom, not fear.

Truth realigns your vision. It steadies your heart. It anchors you in what God says instead of what circumstances scream.

This is why the enemy works overtime to distort truth in your mind. If he can distort what you see, he can distract where you go.

But when you're armed with truth, you move differently. You pause before reacting. You ask God for wisdom. You start to realize that if the enemy is working this hard to distract or trap you... there must be something powerful on the other side.

When Knowing Isn't Enough

You can know the enemy sets traps. You can even know God's Word. But if you don't use what you know, you're still vulnerable.

James 1:22 says, *"Be doers of the word, and not hearers only, deceiving yourselves."*

That word *deceiving* is interesting. It means you can trick yourself into thinking you're safe just because you know the truth. But knowledge isn't protection unless you apply it.

Recognizing the setup is step one. But rejecting the bait, resisting the lie, and replacing it with truth—that's what turns the tide.

What You Don't Know *Can* Hurt You

We've all heard the phrase, *"What you don't know can't hurt you."* Spiritually, nothing could be further from the truth.

Hosea 4:6 says, *"My people are destroyed for lack of knowledge: because thou hast rejected knowledge, I will also reject thee, that thou shalt be no priest to me: seeing thou hast forgotten the law of thy God, I will also forget thy children."*

Ignorance leaves you open. It makes you more susceptible to setups because you don't see them coming. That's why understanding how the enemy works is so vital—it's not about being fearful; it's about being informed and equipped.

God never designed you to walk through life unaware and unarmed. He wants you wise, discerning, and steady—especially when bad news hits.

God's Setup for Your Victory

Here's the plot twist the enemy never sees coming: while he's setting up your downfall, God is setting you up for a comeback.

Joseph was thrown into a pit, sold into slavery, and falsely imprisoned. From the outside, it looked like a total defeat. But it was all a divine setup. Every step led him closer to the palace — and eventually, to saving an entire nation.

The same is true for you. What looks like sabotage may be a setup for significance. What looks like a loss may be a launchpad for your next season.

Romans 8:28 says, *"And we know that in all things God works for the good of those who love him, who have been called according to his purpose."*

The enemy may have a plan — but God has the final move.

Final Thoughts

Bad news doesn't have to take you out.

When you understand that the enemy sets traps — but God sets *you* up for victory — everything changes. You stop reacting in fear and start responding in faith. You begin to see beyond the surface and trust that even this, even now, is not the end of your story.

There is a setup. But it's not for your downfall. It's for your breakthrough. It's for your victory. It's part of what makes you *Unshakeable*.

You've been set up by God for victory—not taken down by the enemy's schemes.

Stay Unshakeable.

Power In Proactivity

It was a bitterly cold winter day in New England several years ago. After an evening away, a friend and I stayed overnight at a Newport, Rhode Island hotel. The following day, we took a scenic drive along the coast, enjoying the sunlight sparkling on the calm sea and glistening like crystals on the snowy ground.

Still feeling the chill from the brisk coastal air, we were eager for a warm meal when we pulled into a well-known inn famous for its hearty brunches. The cozy dining room offered a warm welcome with the crackling warmth of a fireplace and our linen-lined table for two overlooking the breathtaking Atlantic coast. A pianist played softly in the background, adding to the ambiance.

Just as we had ordered our meal, the hotel where I worked called. The employee on the line was anxious—the pipes had burst, and water was everywhere! So much for the serenity of the moment. Despite the limited staff on duty at the hotel that quiet January morning, the staff managed to get a plumber out to apply a temporary fix until the next day.

The bigger question was — why did this happen? The hotel had faced this issue before, and there were clear procedures to prevent it. Yet someone had neglected those steps on one of the coldest weekends of the year.

That moment revealed something deeper: As the hotel's general manager then, I realized that many of the problems managers brought to me — whether with their team or about the building itself — could have been avoided with one key action: **being proactive.** Time after time, costly issues could have been prevented if someone had taken the necessary steps beforehand.

Proactivity in Spiritual Life

So, what does being proactive have to do with handling bad news? Everything.

Life's hardships may not come in the form of burst pipes, but unexpected challenges often hit with the same chaotic force. While we can't always prevent trouble, being proactive spiritually can position us to be prepared, standing in faith, and not shaken.

The opposite of being proactive is being reactive. When bad news catches us off guard, we tend to scramble — trying to pray, believe, or declare God's promises in a state of panic. While God is merciful and meets us where we are, there's a better way: building a foundation of faith before the storm hits.

For example, one of the principles we've discussed in this book is to "resist fear." But we allow fear to quietly take root in small moments when we worry about finances, family, or health. In that case, it's harder to exercise authority over it when a major crisis arises.

I once knew a couple who faced overwhelming financial trouble. This couple had fallen behind on their mortgage, and after months without payment, the bank set a foreclosure date. Understandably, they were devastated. When the bank came to take their home in the morning, one of them desperately prayed for a miracle — for God to somehow provide the entire overdue amount.

My heart ached for them, but I couldn't help but think: *If they had struggled to believe in God for one month's mortgage, how could they suddenly believe in a sum many times greater?* Their faith had not been worked in the smaller amounts, making it harder to trust God when faced with more significant amount of debt.

This is true in financial matters and every area of life. When we've spent time with God daily — learning His Word, listening for His voice, and building our trust in Him — we're prepared to stand firm when bad news comes.

David's Proactive Faith

This principle shines clearly in David's life.

When David faced Goliath, he boldly declared that God would deliver the Philistine into his hand. But notice what prepared David for this moment:

"Your servant has killed both the lion and the bear; this uncircumcised Philistine will be like one of them... The Lord who rescued me from the paw of the lion and the paw of the bear will rescue me from the hand of this Philistine." (1 Samuel 17:36-37)

David's victory over Goliath wasn't random — it resulted from a proactive relationship with God that had already been proven in the quiet training grounds of faith. Long before Goliath threatened Israel, David had already faced battles. David had fought off predators in the wilderness alone with his father's sheep.

But even before those victories, David had built a deeper foundation — a life of daily fellowship with God. Scripture tells us that David was "a man after God's own heart" (1

Samuel 13:14). That kind of closeness doesn't happen overnight. David had spent time in God's presence, learning His ways and trusting His character. Because David knew God intimately, he could face Goliath with complete confidence.

But David didn't just know God personally—he also understood his covenant with Him. He knew what belonged to him as a child of Israel and what God had promised His people. That's why when he faced Goliath, he wasn't intimidated. While everyone else saw a giant, David saw an outsider to the covenant—an uncircumcised Philistine with no divine backing.

It wasn't about Goliath's size, skill, or strength. It was about his lack of covenant. Circumcision, in David's day, was the physical mark of God's covenant with Israel—a reminder that they were His people and He was their God. By calling Goliath "uncircumcised," David wasn't just stating a fact—he was making a legal declaration. Goliath had no right to defy the armies of the living God. David knew covenant people had rights to protection, victory, and divine intervention.

David understood covenant talk because he spent time with his covenant God. His understanding of what was rightfully his brought the confidence and assurance that started long before Goliath. Being familiar with what belonged to him and what God would do in the dangerous feat ahead enabled him to remain Unshakeable despite Goliath's significant intimidation. When we know who we are and what we have in Christ, we will remain anchored when Goliath tries to dictate our downfall.

In the same way, the same God who made a covenant with David made a better one with us. Jesus sealed a new covenant for us with His blood. Because of Jesus, we have a covenant relationship with God that carries even greater promises. Just as David knew his covenant rights and refused to be intimidated, we can stand firm when we know what belongs to us through Christ. Healing, peace, provision, and victory aren't just hopeful ideas — they are blood-bought rights Jesus secured for us.

David didn't just wake up one day with fearless faith; he cultivated it by spending time with God in quiet moments. In those still hours, David learned to hear God's voice, trust His leading, learn about his covenant, and see His power in smaller victories. The bear and the lion didn't just prepare David physically; they also prepared him spiritually to trust God no matter the size of the threat.

Notice that David didn't just react to Goliath's threats — he **responded** in faith. While others cowered in fear, David activated his trust in God with his words:

"You come to me with a sword and spear... but I come to you in the name of the Lord of Hosts..." (1 Samuel 17:45)

David's declaration wasn't empty courage — it flowed from a consistent fellowship with God. That same principle applies to us. When bad news strikes, our daily walk with God stabilizes us.

Winning Before the Game

We see this principle of preparation play out even in modern-day examples. While not spiritual, the concept of getting ready *before* the pressure hits is powerfully illustrated in the life of Tom Brady, an American professional football player who played in the NFL for 23 seasons. He became the winningest quarterback in NFL history and is widely regarded as the greatest quarterback of all time and one of the greatest athletes in sports history.

But Brady wasn't born this way. His success wasn't just about raw talent — it was built in the unseen hours, long before he stepped onto the field. Tom Brady studied plays, practiced relentlessly, and mentally rehearsed victory. When the odds were against him, he refused to quit. Despite being overlooked in the early draft rounds, he held onto hope — and when his opportunity finally came, he was the 199th overall pick.

What set Brady apart wasn't just his ability on game day; it was the preparation he had put in behind the scenes. He had already won the battle in his mind long before the game began. So, when the moment arrived, he didn't panic — he performed with precision. Likewise, proactive faith isn't just about reacting in crisis; it's about preparing your heart and mind ahead of time.

I've experienced this principle in my own life. There have been times when I sensed the Holy Spirit leading me to pray, knowing something was coming down the road. The Holy Spirit is all about being proactive. Jesus promised in John 16:13 that the Spirit would *"show us things to come."* I didn't always understand what was ahead at the time, but I knew God was preparing me. And when those moments arrived, because I had followed His leading in prayer, I wasn't caught off guard or overwhelmed with panic — I was already equipped to walk through it with faith.

It is winning *before* the fight.

Daily Proactive Goals

We can learn a lot from David's proactive actions. His strength didn't come from one grand moment of faith—it was built through consistent, daily actions. Developing proactive faith doesn't require giant leaps but small steps taken consistently each day.

If we establish daily habits that anchor us in God's presence, we won't be shaken when life's storms come. So, what are some practical actions we can incorporate into our lives?

Immerse Yourself in the Word: Beyond reading a few verses, look for ways to saturate your day with God's Word. Listen to a sermon from a trusted teacher on a podcast, read a book that unpacks Scripture, or set aside time to study a specific passage. The more we know God's Word, the more confidence we'll have in His promises, bringing hope and assurance no matter what we face.

Meditate on Scripture: Meditation is a powerful way to engrain God's truth in your heart. Take a single verse, like Psalm 91:1— "He that dwelleth in the secret place of the Most High shall abide under the shadow of the Almighty." Find a quiet place, repeat it softly, and let each word sink in. Picture yourself under God's protective shadow. Over time, this practice will transform your thinking, filling your heart with faith and peace.

Quiet Time with God: Set aside sacred moments to be with the Father—no requests, no agenda, just being with Him. In those quiet moments, He will bring peace to your heart, remind you of His promises, and give you practical wisdom for challenges you face. Learning to rest in His presence strengthens your ability to hear His voice and trust His leading.

Just as David's faith was strengthened one day at a time, we can develop proactive faith by intentionally practicing these habits. Think of it as your Faith Toolbox—tools you sharpen daily so they're ready when the enemy wants to challenge us. By consistently using these tools, you'll build a reservoir of strength that steadies you when life's battles arise. When life shakes, you won't have to scramble for faith—you'll already be standing on solid ground.

Building Your Foundation

If we've spent time with Jesus—learning His Word, hearing His voice, and resting in His presence—we'll have confidence when trials arise. We'll know, beyond a doubt, that He is our Shepherd, Provider, Healer, and Peace.

Victory doesn't start in the battle — it begins in the quiet moments with God and his Word. Being proactive.

The enemy's threats may roar like Goliath, shouting intimidation and fear. But when we've been with Jesus, we can stand firm and declare with confidence:

"I know my God — and through Him I have the victory."

What are you doing today to prepare your heart for tomorrow's challenges? Are you feeding your spirit with God's Word? Are you practicing *covenant talk* and filling your mouth with His promises? Like David, you can build a foundation that will hold you steady when Goliath shouts his threats, and like Tom Brady, you can be ready for game day.

So today, don't wait until trouble comes. Build your faith now. Spend time with God now. Start today. The victory is won before the fight ever starts. And when you've walked with Him daily, you won't crumble when the enemy shouts — you'll respond with Unshakeable confidence in the One who has never failed.

Be Proactive – Be Unshakeable

Don't Panic – Turn inside

Panic is real.

It doesn't wait for your permission. It doesn't knock politely—it rushes in like a wave. Your heart races, thoughts scatter, and your breath shortens. Panic hijacks peace and floods the mind, leaving you dizzy with fear and unable to find your footing.

A phone call, diagnosis, accident, or headline can trigger panic. Panic spins so fast it drowns out the truth. It's when external noise becomes internal chaos. And it shouts, *"React now! You're not safe!"*

But what if there's a better response?

What if, instead of reacting outwardly, we learned to turn inward—not to ignore the situation, but to listen for the One who is steady when everything else shakes?

Just as the body uses breathing or grounding techniques to stabilize the nervous system, your spirit has its stabilizer: the voice of the Holy Spirit within. *Panic wants a reaction. But the Spirit invites a response.*

The more profound truth is that you're not helpless in the storm. The Spirit of God lives inside you. And when panic tries to rise, the most powerful move you can make is to *look inside your spirit to hear the Spirit's leadings, that still small voice.*

Turning inward isn't escapism. It's re-centering on truth. It's not denial—it's divine alignment.

A Real-Life Storm

Driving home from work one afternoon, I encountered a serious car accident. I wasn't in a hurry, so I pulled over to help. Approaching one of the vehicles, a man stepped out—his shirt and shoes were stained with blood, and he was bleeding from his head. The other car was mangled. Someone was trapped inside.

People began to gather. Sirens wailed. Police and firefighters swarmed the scene. The fire captain barked orders—"Get another truck!" "Call for ambulances!" EMTs worked on the injured man while the firefighters used the jaws of life to cut open the crushed metal.

Sirens. Shouting. Flashing lights. Chaos everywhere.

And isn't that exactly what panic feels like?

That's what it's like when we get unexpected news. Our emotions scream, our hearts pound and our thoughts go wild. It's a full-body experience—fear, shock, confusion, helplessness—and everything is falling apart.

It reminds me of Elijah on Mount Horeb. First, a mighty wind tore through the mountains. Then came an earthquake. Then fire. But God wasn't in any of those. He was in the still, small voice—the whisper.

We can become so skilled at turning to our spirit in moments of crisis that His still, small voice becomes the *loudest* voice—even amid panic. That whisper can bring answers, stability, strategy, and hope.

No situation—no matter how intense—can stop the Holy Spirit from speaking. But if we're not careful, panic can keep *us* from listening. That's why it's so essential to practice turning inward—to recognize when panic takes over and respond by tuning into the still, steady voice of the Spirit.

Don't panic. Turn inside.

What does that mean?

It means turning your attention to your spirit. Ask yourself:

- What is the Holy Spirit leading me to do?
- Where is the peace?
- What is He speaking?

We've gone over this in more detail in another chapter—but here, in panic, this is where truth anchors you.

And yet—the answer—is in your spirit, where God Himself lives and speaks. *John 2:20 says, "But you have an unction from the Holy One, and you know everything."*

Just like I stopped to help the injured person at the scene of the accident, God stopped to help *you* in your crisis. He doesn't turn away. He moves toward you—to lead, speak, and steady you with His peace.

I once heard a story about a preacher swimming in the ocean with a friend. Suddenly, the friend was pulled under by a rip current. He began to panic and thrash, unable to think clearly. The preacher tried to help, but the man's wild movements put them both in danger.

So, the preacher did the unthinkable. He slapped him—not out of anger, but to snap him out of panic long enough to pull him to safety. That moment of clarity saved them both.

That's what panic does. It blocks the very help trying to reach us—not because God isn't speaking, but because *we aren't listening.*

Panic may seem like a natural response, but that's all it is—a reaction. It doesn't solve the problem. We cannot let panic dominate our decision-making or dictate our response. There's a better way: turn inside to your spirit.

Because the Holy Spirit is not in a panic. He's not overwhelmed. He's not caught off guard. He is in complete peace—and He is ready to help you.

The Deeper Message: Jesus Looked Inside

We looked at this moment more closely in the chapter on peace—but there's something else worth noticing here. In Mark 4, the disciples panicked during the storm… but Jesus? He was asleep in the boat. When they woke Him, He didn't react to the waves. He responded from within.

His peace wasn't tied to the weather. It was anchored in the Presence within Him.

When the waves are high, don't look at the water—look inside. Peace isn't out there. Peace is already in you.

Don't panic—turn inside.

You've learned throughout this book how God speaks:

- Through peace
- Through the inward witness
- Through the voice of the Holy Spirit inside you

But in the moment of crisis, *you have to apply it.*

When the report is terrible, something unexpected happens, and life flips upside down.

What do you do?

Pause. Breathe deep. Pray in the Spirit. You get quiet. And you turn inside.

When we resist the urge to react—to anxiety, pressure, urgency, intimidation—we create space to hear something entirely different:

The voice of peace. The whisper of wisdom. The still, small voice that *knows the way forward. The inward knowing—* knowing just what to do.

Training for the Storms

You might ask, "How in the world do I train for a storm?"

Like anything else that doesn't come naturally, *we can train to turn inside to hear what the Spirit says.* And the day-to-day moments are the perfect training ground.

It might not be a life-altering crisis, but panic creeps in when:

- You make a costly mistake at work.
- Your dog runs away.
- You get an overdraft notice and don't know how to make it to payday.

These are moments to recognize panic—and *turn inside.* You get stronger each time you reach for what's in your spirit rather than spiraling into fear. You become more skilled at responding, not reacting. It starts to become second nature.

You'll learn to go for the whisper like someone trained to reach for the EpiPen in a life-or-death crisis. For the inward witness. For the voice of peace.

We don't need Google when things feel impossible; we need God.

And when we resist panic, we *will* hear His words, His leading, His peace that stills the chaos and calms the raging sea.

Don't panic—turn inside.

        That's how you stay *Unshakeable.*

The Waiting Period or The Weighting Period?

We've all faced those moments—the agonizing wait after a test, a doctor's visit, or an interview—when questions with no answers fill our minds.

It was May of 1980. The requirement to graduate from Our Redeemer Lutheran High School in Lunalilo, Hawaii, was to pass the English test. This was a big challenge for me. Unfortunately, during my senior year, my studies took second, third, or even fourth place in the bustling life of activities at school and work. I was president of the pep club, a varsity volleyball team member, and part of the religious team council. My sister and I lived in an apartment and worked as waitresses at Farrell's, a popular Honolulu restaurant known for its ice cream sundaes and lively birthday celebrations. Late nights working wasn't the best recipe for success in school, but I loved to work.

So, passing an English test days before school ended was quite the task. But it had to be done... somehow. The only way would be to stay up all night for several nights on end to cram for this test. Fortunately, I was blessed with a photographic memory and was skilled at retention ... when I paid attention. I crammed all night. There were no Starbucks or Dunkin' Donuts as teenagers, so coffee wasn't an option. But they did have a supplement called No Doze, which became my source of strength in ensuring that I could stay awake during those several days. It paid off.

Then, the test day came, and after that, the waiting period. It was an entire time of waiting with questions with no answers. Did I pass or not? What would happen if I didn't pass? Pictures of not graduating with my class in utter humiliation filled my mind, not to mention the disappointment from my dad. I wouldn't be able to deliver the religious speech I had been asked to give during graduation, and my summer would be filled with summer school. The repercussions of not graduating seemed grim.

I remember trying to distract myself, but the questions surfaced: *What if I don't make it? What if all my hard work wasn't enough?* Waiting felt like a mountain of pressure, one I couldn't escape.

Thankfully, I passed the English test, delivered the religious speech at the graduation ceremony, and walked across the stage with my high school diploma. Phew, I made it!

The Waiting Period

The waiting period is the distance between what you know now... and what you'll know next—between the moment you learn something might happen and the moment you find out if it actually will.

It's waiting for test results that could confirm or deny a cancer diagnosis. It's the anxious period when you're hoping a loved one will pull through surgery. It's the uncertainty after your company announces layoffs, wondering if your name is on the list. It's waiting by the phone after a job interview, wondering if you'll hear back. Because our lives move in seasons, waiting is often unavoidable. And sometimes, waiting feels heavier than the answer itself— even if the outcome is favorable.

This is the waiting period. That stretch of time where it seems as though we are at the mercy of the unknown. In this space, time drags. Minutes feel like hours, and our thoughts spiral. Fear whispers scenarios that grow darker the longer we sit with them. The questions are endless: How will this affect my life, family, and job? What if it is fatal? How are we going to make it?

But when you think about it, we wait for things daily. We wait at red lights, we wait in line at the grocery store, we wait for our morning coffee at the drive-thru, and we wait for dinner to finish in the oven. Waiting is woven into our daily lives.

So, what makes waiting for a diagnosis feel so different from waiting at a red light?

The Weight During the Wait

The difference is the **weight** we carry during the **wait**. Waiting at a red light might stir up impatience, but we're not gripped with fear. Waiting for medical results, though? That's a different kind of wait—one that presses on your chest, messes with your sleep, and plays mind games with your peace. It's not just time passing—it's time *heavy* with uncertainty.

But must the waiting period always feel heavy? Do we have to become servants to the "what ifs"- those nagging, spiraling fears that try to rule our thoughts in uncertain times? Does this time have to be filled with anxiety and dread while we are at the mercy of a result or an unknown future?

No, absolutely not!

One Sunday at church, the Lord spoke, "*You are waiting for something to happen, but instead wait on Me.*" He reminded us not to be preoccupied with waiting for that *thing* to settle the issue but to fix our hearts on Him.

Wait on me. Spend time in His presence. Minister to Him, and let Him minister to you. We don't have to wait like the world waits. We're not subject to the grief and fear that come from staring into the unknown. We know the One who holds the outcome, and He's not hiding from us during the visit.

The world will tell you it's normal to feel anxious and burdened with fear during the waiting period. Worry and dread are seen as inevitable when you're at the mercy of unknown results. But this does not have to be your reality for a born-again child of God.

Jesus never intended for you to live in a mental holding cell while outcomes are being worked out. He said, *"They are not of the world, even as I am not of the world." (John 17:16).* Because of what Jesus has done for you, you don't have to think or react like the world does in uncertain situations.

You are not a victim of the wait. Why? Because we've read the back of the Book — and we win. We're not subject to *what might happen* but to the unchanging Word of God. His Word says we are more than conquerors. It says we already have the victory, that we are carriers of peace that surpasses all understanding, and that the Holy Spirit lives within us — revealing things to come.

Jesus knew there would be waiting periods when the enemy would try to flood our minds with fear. But He made a way for us to stand firm. Through Christ, we are overcomers. And because of that, we have authority over the waiting period — ***it doesn't have authority over us.*** We don't have to live by emotional default, reacting to fear, dread, or despair. We can live by faith — steady, anchored, and Unshakeable — even when the outcome isn't yet clear.

The Enemy's Greatest Tool

Fear is Satan's most significant tool in the waiting period. If you surrender to it, you allow him to shape your perspective, fill your mind with lies, and influence your emotional state. But you don't have to give him that power. Instead, God has given you everything you need to resist fear and stand firm.

Romans 8:31 (AMPC) says:

"What then shall we say to all this? If God is for us, who (can be) against us? (Who can be our foe if God is on our side?)"

And Romans 8:37-39 (AMPC) declares:

"Yet amid all these things, we are more than conquerors and gain a surpassing victory through Him who loved us... nothing else in all creation will be able to separate us from the love of God, which is in Christ Jesus our Lord."

II Timothy 1:7 reminds us:

"For God has not given us a spirit of fear, but of power, and of love and of a sound mind."

God is for you — and because of that, there is no reason to be afraid. Fear thrives on worst-case scenarios and exaggerated outcomes, but faith reminds you that God is with you and you already have victory in Him.

The God who conquered death, hell, and the grave is on your side. You are an heir of God and a joint heir with Christ. You rule and reign with Him — and that means you are not subject to the torment that fear, dread, and anxiety try to bring.

God has given you the power to stand **Unshakeable** in the middle of the waiting period. He has equipped you with tools to resist the enemy's tactics — tools that silence intimidation, shut down trepidation, and overpower overwhelming sorrow.

The enemy may try to fill your mind with *deafening whispers of fear*, but those whispers are no match for the mighty force of the Holy Spirit within you. The first step is to recognize this: anxiety is not your normal as a believer. Your mind and emotions can remain in perfect peace — free from anxiety, fret, or worry. And as a believer, peace is your normal. Don't ever let anyone convince you otherwise.

So, when the enemy tries to intimidate and knock you down with fear, telling you how your future will be, speak to the fear and command fear to go in Jesus' name! (We will cover more of this in the *Resist Fear* chapter.)

This isn't wishful thinking — it's just another victorious day in the life of a believer who refuses to surrender to the enemy's plan.

The Cause: Your Thought Life

What causes emotions like worry, apprehension and fear to flare up? Often, it's not the situation itself — the thoughts that follow and the influence those thoughts bring.

As a young child, every Sunday after church, we had a routine. We'd go home, change our clothes, put our German Shepherd, Lady, in the truck, and head to Grandma's house for a home-cooked Sunday dinner.

Sunday dinners were hearty—fried chicken, mashed potatoes with gravy, fried okra — and my favorite — fried peach pies with homemade vanilla ice cream. Those golden peach pies with fresh peaches tucked inside the made-from-scratch crust, smothered with butter, are still vivid in my memory — and my taste buds! Just thinking about those foods brings back fond memories and a hunger for fried peach pies!

Thoughts are powerful. They stir emotions, whether positive or negative. And thoughts are also very influential. If we think about a hot fudge sundae for too long, we will get in our car and drive to get one! Too often, though, we don't take control of our thoughts, and we let thoughts of the wrong kind, fear, and doubt slip in unnoticed—and they start to grow.

It's your *thoughts* that determine your emotional response. If your mind never whispered, *"What if it's cancer?"* or *"What if I lose my job and can't afford treatment?"* you probably wouldn't think twice about what the results could be.

Your thought life is where the real battle lies. The enemy knows this….do you?

Escape the Waiting Period – Win the Battle in Your Mind

Paul writes in 2 Corinthians 10:3-5 (AMPC):

"For though we walk (live) in the flesh, we are not carrying on our warfare according to the flesh and using mere human weapons. For the weapons of our warfare are not physical (weapons of flesh and blood), but they are mighty before God for the overthrow and destruction of strongholds. (Since we) refute arguments and theories and reasonings and every proud and lofty thing that sets itself up against the (true)

knowledge of God; and we lead every thought and purpose away captive into the obedience of Christ (the Messiah, the Anointed One)."

The *pulling down of strongholds* in this passage refers to overcoming spiritual obstacles—the ones that rise up in one's mind during uncertain moments.

Jesus promised us peace, but the enemy will always attempt to resist that peace. His strategy is simple but effective: steal your peace and confidence in God by slipping into your thoughts unnoticed. His whispers are often subtle—quiet enough to seem harmless yet powerful enough to grow into destructive patterns if left unchecked.

I didn't master this principle during the three weeks before my testing. I wish I could say it was handled it perfectly, but it was not. Busy at work and traveling out of state, allowed subtle thoughts to slip in. Thoughts that should have been examined, but were not. I entertained them without even realizing it—and then the fear came.

It wasn't loud or obvious. The thoughts didn't come shouting, *"What if you have cancer again?"* Instead, they whispered. They were casual little thoughts that felt harmless at first. But as I let them stay, they began to snowball, and apprehension and a lack of peace soon followed.

In hindsight, it's obvious now how minute those thoughts were—but also that I didn't have to let those thoughts stay. The enemy is sly. This is a reminder to guard our minds intentionally, especially during a waiting time.

The enemy's strategy has been to plant seeds of doubt and fear. Thoughts are like seeds — if you let them settle and stay, they will grow.

That's why setting a guard over your mind is so crucial. The battle isn't just about what *might* happen in the future — the real fight is over what you allow to take root in your mind right now.

If you allow fearful thoughts to linger, they'll gain momentum and try to overpower your confidence in Christ. But if you resist them, you'll retain the power and authority that already belongs to you in Him. Take authority over those thoughts and the fear that comes with them by *speaking to those thoughts*. If a thought comes, *"you will die of cancer,"* speak God's Word back to that thought saying, *"I rebuke that thought in Jesus' name. I shall live and not die!"* And while you are at it, rebuke the fear that comes with it!

Fearful thoughts don't just leave just because you ignore them or try to think about something else. You must address them – and speak to them. Don't let the enemy toss you around with fear. Use your God-given authority. Resist him

Think on Purpose...For Peace

When troubling thoughts try to take over, resisting them is only half the battle—you must also replace them.

Isaiah 26:3 promises, *"Thou wilt keep him in perfect peace whose mind is stayed on thee."*

Notice that peace doesn't come by simply wishing those anxious thoughts away. Peace comes when your mind is intentionally anchored on God and His promises.

When the enemy does his utmost to overwhelm you with despair, God's Word becomes your shield — pushing back the fear and filling your heart with peace.

That's why meditating on Scripture during those anxious moments is so powerful. Just as destructive thoughts can drag you into worry, right thoughts can lift you into peace that surpasses understanding.

And remember — when you meditate on God's Word, it's not just ink on a page. It's living power flowing into your mind — the very breath of God calming your heart and restoring your peace.

Throw ALL Your Care Away

1 Peter 5:7 (AMPC) says:

"Casting the whole of your care [all your anxieties, all your worries, all your concerns, once and for all] on Him, for He cares for you affectionately and cares about you watchfully."

Here's another powerful tool God has given us to maintain peace when the enemy tries to overwhelm us with despair: casting all our care on Him. You are not required to carry the weight of what the enemy brings. You have a promise—one of peace, confidence, and assurance.

But what does that look like? It's an intentional, faith-filled act. When those nagging thoughts come — *"What if...?"* or *"But what about...?"* — God's Word tells us exactly what to do: Cast ALL your care on him. Don't carry the weight. You can pray like this:

"Father, in the name of Jesus, I cast all this care on You. I refuse to carry it. Your Word says You care for me, and You will take it. I do not have to hold onto it so that I will release it to you now."

You may have to say *"I cast my care onto the Lord,"* this repeatedly because the enemy doesn't give up easily. He'll try again and again to lure you back into anxiety. But you are **not powerless** in those moments. *Philippians 4:13 declares: "I can do all things through Christ who strengthens me."*

The enemy wants you to default to fear — to let negative thoughts and worst-case scenarios take over. He'll use voices around you, stories of bad outcomes, and waves of panic to shake your faith. But you are not at his mercy.

Instead, you can:

- Speak to fear and resist it
- Cast down wrong imaginations and speak to those thoughts
- Replace those thoughts with God's Word
- Cast all your cares on the Lord

This is God's powerful recipe for peace in the waiting period—so effective that you will find yourself saying, *"Wait... what **weighting** period?"* The enemy brings weight, God brings peace.

Pray In The Spirit

Praying in the Spirit is one of the most important things you can do in the waiting period.

Any emotion that tries to overtake you can be overtaken by praying in the Spirit. This cannot be emphasized enough. When the enemy is painting a hopeless picture, pray in the Spirit. When dread, uncertainty are knocking at your door, and grief is trying to settle in with thoughts of tragedy, pray in the Spirit.

It builds you up on the inside, strengthening your spirit and opening your heart to God's comfort, strategy and direction. When your spirit is strong, it flows over into the natural realm—bringing supernatural peace and calm. And it keeps emotions down and thoughts from racing—on the what ifs.

This is discussed more fully in the chapter, *What To Do When You Don't Know What to Do.*

That Won't Work!

God's Word often gives us strategies that seem almost too simple. And isn't that just like human nature to assume that the more challenging path must be the better one.

My uncle used to tell me, "Kat, you always do things the hard way!" One time, I spent hours troubleshooting a computer issue. I researched everything and tried every trick—nothing worked. Finally, I called my manager. He walked over, pressed one simple button, and said, "Try that."

I doubted it — surely it couldn't be *that* easy. But sure enough, the solution came. That simple step wasn't the whole fix, but it got things moving in the right direction.

God's Word is like that. Simple — but powerful.

The enemy will try to convince you that the instructions in God's Word are too basic to work in your situation. *"Casting your care? Quoting Scripture? That won't fix this."* But he knows better — because he knows the power released when you obey God's instructions.

It's not about how complicated the solution is — it's about how powerful obedience is when rooted in God's Word.

Winning In The Every Day

These tools aren't perfected when we receive bad news — they're strengthened daily.

It's in ordinary moments that we build spiritual habits:

- Watching what enters our mind
- Consistently filling our thoughts with God's thoughts
- Meditating on His Word — not dwelling on what the enemy tries to bring
- Speak to fear and command it to go in the little things
- Praying in the Spirit daily and during the small challenges
- When something disturbs you, unsettles you, or keeps your mind spinning — don't let it linger. Cast it on the Lord.

It's those daily choices that fortify us when the enemy comes.

Waiting Without The Weight

Maybe you've endured the anxiety and discomfort of the waiting period, thinking it was just an unavoidable part of life — something you had to suffer through.

But now you know the truth: as a child of God, you are not subject to hopeless waiting seasons where fear and uncertainty steal your peace.

In Christ Jesus, you are equipped with everything you need to overcome. You've been given powerful tools — God's Word, promises, and presence — and you have authority and victory over the unsettledness of the wait. We can choose to wait on the Lord, cast our care on him, and stand guard at the entrance of our minds, pray in the Spirit and use our authority over fear and thoughts. This keeps us from falling into the enemy's trap of fear and despair.

Being Unshakeable...Weight Free

The Mind of a Champion

It was a cold, snowy February day in New Hampshire. My then-husband and I had rented a condo in the mountains for a brief getaway. Though it was only a short trip, we were both looking forward to some rest and the chance to enjoy something different from the usual routine.

The condo was a charming split-level with a winding staircase leading to a cozy bedroom that offered a breathtaking view of the snow-covered mountains stretching far and wide. On the first level, the open kitchen with a breakfast bar became our gathering place, where we enjoyed home-cooked meals and unrushed conversations—reflecting on the day behind us and anticipating the adventures ahead. The warmth of the fireplace added to the serene atmosphere, making it the perfect retreat.

The next day, we decided to try a classic winter activity—skiing. Neither of us had skied before, so we wisely signed up for a lesson. Fortunately, being midweek, the resort was nearly empty, which made the experience far less intimidating.

Our instructor was patient and knowledgeable, guiding us through the essential techniques. By the end of the lesson, we felt confident enough to tackle the beginner slopes. But my then-husband had bigger ambitions. He was convinced we could handle more than just the gentle, forgiving trails—he wanted to take on one of the highest peaks.

Apprehensive but trusting, I followed him, believing his assumption that it wouldn't be too difficult. I soon discovered just how wrong that assumption was.

Conquering the Descent through Focus

Getting off the ski lift was a challenge in itself! I remember thinking there should be a lesson dedicated solely to that task.

But the real test came once we were on the slope, not just any hill. This route felt like the Mount Everest of ski runs for a first-time skier. The drop to the bottom seemed impossibly steep. Was there a lift that could take me straight to the end? No. It was just me on my skis.

As we cautiously started forward, I quickly realized this was no leisurely glide down a gentle hill. The speed picked up almost instantly, and before I knew it, I wasn't skiing—I was racing. It felt like I had been dropped onto a NASCAR speedway, except I had no steering wheel, brakes, or a way to escape. This was survival of the fittest, and I was a rookie thrown into the end.

The slope was an open white expanse with no trees or other skiers. But that didn't make it any less terrifying. The sheer velocity made it painfully clear: this could end badly. My then-husband was of no help—he was in the same predicament. And at this speed, even attempting a controlled fall, like I'd learned in ice skating, wasn't an option.

As the ground beneath me blurred, fear suddenly shifted to focus. Every ounce of my attention zeroed in on one thing—the instructions from our ski instructor. *Keep your knees bent. Look straight ahead.* That was all that mattered. My mind fought to wander, but I forced myself to stay locked in. If I let my thoughts stray for a second, the outcome could be drastically different.

Then came the next challenge—stopping. The end of the slope was fast approaching. My focus shifted again, this time to remembering exactly *how* to stop. Bracing myself, I attempted the technique we had learned. And much to my shock, it worked! I skidded to a successful stop, still in one piece.

At the bottom of the hill, our ski instructor stood watching, his expression a mix of surprise and relief. A few others had gathered, likely drawn in by the spectacle of two skiers barreling down the steep mountain. I wanted to hug our instructor out of sheer gratitude. I had just survived what felt like an impossible challenge—and done without a single injury. Indeed, God's angels were with me.

The Focused Aftermath

My then-husband's experience, however, was a different story. As we stood waiting for him to appear, we suddenly caught sight of his body flipping in a full circle through the air before crashing to the ground. For a moment, we weren't sure if he'd even be able to get up. Falling on snow might look soft, but it's like hitting solid ice.

After what felt like forever, we finally saw him descending the slope. Thankfully, nothing was seriously injured—except, perhaps, his ego. And to be fair, that was well deserved for convincing me to tackle the highest peak!

That evening, as we sat by the fireplace at a nearby restaurant, thawing out with clam chowder and steaming cocoa, the reality of what had just happened sank in. Looking back on that harrowing yet exhilarating experience, one thing stood out: I had made it down that mountain because my focus had locked in tenaciously, following every instruction to the letter. I may not have been an Olympic skier that day, but my mind had operated like a champion athlete—with laser-sharp concentration and determination.

And ultimately, all the thanks and gratitude belonged to the Lord. Without His divine help—placing us with the right instructor, blessing us with a clear day, granting us the ability to focus, and surrounding us with angels—this story could have had a different ending.

Definition of Focus

Focus.

This powerful verb means to direct one's attention toward something with intention and precision. In *The Power of Focus* by Jack Canfield, the author states that the number one reason people fail to achieve their goals is a lack of focus. Professional athletes understand this well—their success or failure often hinges on their ability to remain focused under pressure.

Developing Focus – The Champion's Mindset

Take Olympic gymnasts, for example. Watching the gymnasts compete in the 2024 Olympics was a masterclass in focus. One slight misstep—a foot landing an inch too far to the left—could jeopardize an entire routine and shatter years of training, discipline, and sacrifice. Their minds must be locked in, allowing no room for distraction until the routine is complete. This kind of focus is the mindset of a champion.

But behind their dazzling performances lies a less visible but equally crucial aspect: the rigorous mental training that shapes them into champions. Focus is a skill they must develop long before they step onto the floor, beam, or mat.

Every day, gymnasts train their minds to concentrate, block out distractions, and maintain mental discipline even when the pressure is mounting. This training involves repeating their routines, visualizing success, and committing to unwavering mental clarity.

This kind of mental training is valid for all areas of life. Success doesn't happen by accident. It's built through consistent focus. When we focus on God's Word, His promises, and truth in our everyday lives, we prepare ourselves for the more significant moments when the stakes are higher, and there are many distractions. Developing focus isn't about avoiding distractions but learning how to handle them and push through, just like an athlete who refines their skills in the gym for the big game or competition.

Applying Focus – Performing Under Pressure

Let's look at how focus plays out when it truly matters. Imagine the Olympic gymnasts performing during the final round of competition. There is a world of difference between the training environment and the pressure of the live competition. The stakes are high. The world is watching. They cannot afford to let distractions, fears, or doubts enter their minds.

Under pressure is where applied focus makes all the difference. When the pressure is on, the gymnast's years of mental training come into play. They've spent hours learning how to control their thoughts, manage fear, and lock in their focus. In these moments, they don't have time to think about past mistakes or what might happen if they fail—they focus solely on the task at hand, maintaining a clear mind and confidence in their training.

The same kind of laser focus can be seen in other champions, regardless of their sport. It's not just about the physical skill-it's about mastering the mental game. Consider golf legend Tiger Woods.

Tiger Woods is an American professional golfer with numerous awards naming him the best golfer of all time. He was taught about focus at a very early age. Tiger's father, Earl Woods, didn't just teach him the technical skills of golf; he trained him in the discipline of focus. One of his most effective techniques was intentionally creating distractions—coughing, dropping clubs, or making sudden noises—while Tiger practiced. Instead of letting these disruptions derail him, Tiger learned to tune out the noise and remain locked in on his swing. This mental resilience became one of his greatest assets on the course. Tiger learned that the ability to stay focused amid chaos resulted from deliberate mental training.

Similarly, we must apply focus in times of crisis. When life throws us a curveball—bad news, a challenge, or an unexpected setback—we must recall the mental training we've developed by meditating on God's Word and promises.

The ability to focus on God's truth and the victory He has already secured for us will enable us to overcome distractions and stay strong in the face of adversity.

The Downfall of Distraction

Tiger Woods' ability to block out external chaos on the course is a prime example of how focus can give us a significant edge. But just as the focus has its power, distraction—its opposite—can be equally powerful and often destructive.

Distraction is the enemy of focus. By definition, distraction is anything that diverts attention from what truly matters. And distraction can be dangerous.

Consider the warnings plastered on highway billboards—clever words and striking images urging drivers to put their phones down and focus on the road. It takes only one second of distraction—a glance at a text message—to cause a fatal accident.

I remember driving out of Boston on a Saturday morning on the Massachusetts Turnpike, in the fast lane. I quickly turned to adjust the radio, and when I looked back up the car in front of me was suddenly swerving in and out of the lane. It happened so fast. Thankfully, I had just enough time to brake. Had I been even a few feet closer, it could have caused a major pile-up – all because of a momentary, seemingly minor distraction.

Distractions come in many forms, but their effect is the same: they pull us away from what is essential.

Unshakeable Focus: A Biblical Response to Life's Distractions

Let's look at a biblical example that demonstrates the power of unwavering focus amid opposition: Nehemiah's journey to rebuild the walls of Jerusalem. Nehemiah faced numerous distractions, but his determination to stay focused on God's purpose kept him on track. The Word of God is direct regarding staying focused and providing clear examples of undistracted individuals despite opposition.

Isaiah 50:7 (AMPC)

"For the Lord God helps me; therefore have I not been ashamed or confounded; I have set my face like a flint, and I know that I shall not be put to shame."

Proverbs 4:25-27 (AMPC)

"Let your eyes look right on [with fixed purpose], and let your gaze be straight before you. Consider well the path of your feet, and let all your ways be established and ordered aright. Turn not aside to the right hand or to the left; remove your foot from evil."

These verses emphasize the importance of steadfast focus, urging us to stay fixed on God's plan even when distractions arise. Nehemiah's story is a powerful example of this kind of unwavering focus.

In the book of Nehemiah, we see Nehemiah's passionate commitment to the task at hand. After the Israelites returned from Babylonian captivity, Nehemiah, with permission from King Artaxerxes, set out to rebuild the city's defenses. But the moment progress began, so did the opposition. Led by Sanballat, the enemies of Israel sought to disrupt the work by causing confusion, fear, and sabotage. They attacked Nehemiah's efforts at every turn, but Nehemiah's determination to stay focused on God's purpose kept him moving forward.

Despite relentless attacks, criticism, and fear tactics, the work continued. By Chapter 6, in Nehemiah, only one task remained—setting the doors upon the gates. Yet, Sanballat and his men refused to relent. They devised a final scheme, calling Nehemiah to meet them in the Valley of Ono, intending to harm him.

But Nehemiah refused to be distracted. Notice his response in *Nehemiah 6:3:*

"And I sent messengers unto them, saying, I am doing a great work, so that I cannot come down: why should the work cease, whilst I leave it, and come down to you?"

Had Nehemiah given in to distraction, he would have walked into their trap, been killed, and the wall would have remained unfinished. The wall wasn't just a structure--it represented safety, identity and the future of a people. The enemy's strategy was to lure Nehemiah away, to stop the building and remove the protection.

Likewise, when the enemy threatens to steal our sense of security-whether emotionally, spiritually, or physically we must keep our eyes fixed on the promises and purposes of God. In moments like this focus isn't optional; it's essential.

To better understand how distraction derails us in those critical moments, let's look at three familiar sources of distraction that Nehemiah faced – fear, intimidation, and titles – and how they can steal our focus and shift our attention from God's plan.

Fear

Nehemiah gave the Israelites a clear directive: *Keep your mind on the Lord.* He reminded them that God is great and mighty and that they should not fear the enemy. In essence, Nehemiah was saying: *Do not focus on the enemy—focus on the greatness of God. Draw courage from knowing who He is.*

If they had given into fear—imagining the destruction of their city, the destruction of the wall they were rebuilding and even their families—their focus would have shifted from God to the enemy. And that's precisely what the enemy wanted.

The Bible warns us about the power of fear:

- *Fear has torment.* (1 John 4:18)
- Job said, *"What I feared has come upon me".* (Job 3:25)

Fear is never from God—it is a weapon of the enemy. When threats, bad news, or adverse reports try to distract you, resist fear and hold fast to the promise God gave you for that situation. Fear is one of the enemy's most significant distractions, and we must guard against it. We can walk in peace and confidence when we keep our minds fixed on the Lord.

I experienced this firsthand when I lived in Honolulu, Hawaii, and attended an Assembly of God church. I was very active in the church and had many close friends. One Friday night, I had the opportunity to perform a mime at our singles group. It was a powerful presentation with a strong message, and I had spent the entire week rehearsing. But as the performance drew closer, so did the relentless attacks of fear.

What if so-and-so sees it and doesn't like it?
What if it's a total flop? What if I make a fool of myself?

Like a skiing incident, I faced years later, I had to fight against fearful thoughts and focus solely on the performance. I couldn't think about who was watching or what they might think. Battling fear and distraction took more effort than the actual rehearsals!

Finally, the night of the performance arrived. Once again, I had to focus on the presentation—not on the audience or failure. But because I had already trained myself to focus in my private time, it became more manageable when the pressure was on—right before I stepped onto the stage.

And because my focus was clear, unhindered by fear or distraction, the performance was a complete success!

Intimidation

Nehemiah's enemies tried to intimidate him and his team to stop the work.

Nehemiah 4:8

"And conspired all of them together to come, and to fight against Jerusalem, and hinder it."

Likewise, in times of crisis, the enemy will use intimidation to distract us—whether through thoughts, circumstances or even the responses (or lack thereof) of others. His goal is to shake our confidence, making us question who God is, what He has spoken, and the victory we already have in Him.

But intimidation only has power if we yield to it. If we allow intimidation to take root, it opens the door to fear. And fear, in turn, gives the enemy room to operate and carry out his schemes.

One of the enemy's most excellent tactics is to stop the work of God in and through us. But here's the truth: *his intimidation tactics are powerless unless we allow ourselves to be distracted.* When we stay focused on God, intimidation loses its grip, and the enemy's plans fall apart.

The next time intimidation comes knocking, recognize it for what it is—a distraction meant to steal your focus. Instead of shrinking back from intimidation, focus on what God has said, standing firm in faith and refusing to be moved.

Titles That Threaten

When we think of champions—Olympic gold medalists, Super Bowl winning quarterbacks, or Miss America winners—they all face competitors with powerful titles.

Yet, they don't win by focusing on who they are up against. Their victories come from staying focused on their training, skills, and purpose.

In Nehemiah's time, the men leading the opposition were not just troublemakers; they were officials with titles, in positions of influence, and perceived power. Yet, despite their authority, their titles were not strong enough to stop the plan of God. Nehemiah refused to be distracted by their status. He remained focused on the only power that truly mattered—the power and might of God.

Similarly, when we receive bad news, titles can become a tool of intimidation. A doctor's diagnosis of *cancer*, a financial statement declaring *bankruptcy*, a legal document stating *divorce*—these words carry weight and attempt to paint pictures of loss, defeat, and failure. If we let our minds fixate on the threat behind the title, fear will creep in, and our focus on God's power will weaken.

But no title—no diagnosis, no circumstance, no label—outranks the authority of our God. Psalm 62:11 declares, *"Power belongs to God."* He holds all power, and we, as His children, stand in His authority. His Word and His promises are the highest power in our lives.

When we keep our focus on Him, knowing that the name of Jesus is the highest title, we refuse to let intimidating titles pull us off track.

Philippians 2:9-10

9 *Wherefore God also hath highly exalted him and given him a name which is above every name:*
10 That at the name of Jesus every knee should bow of things in heaven, and things in earth, and things under the earth.

No title is above the name of Jesus. And he has given us the power to use His name against every attack of the enemy. The enemy will try to stir fear through the influence of intimidating titles, pressuring us to put more trust in human voices than in God's Word. But like Nehemiah, we must stand firm, rooted in God's authority, refusing to be shaken.

Directing Our Focus

As we've discussed, distractions will try to pull us away from our focus, but what exactly should we focus on? To stay unshaken, we must define our concentration clearly.

Our focus should be on God's Word—on who we are in Christ, whose we are, and what we have in Him. In the face of bad news, we must focus on His promises in the Scriptures and what He has personally spoken to us.

Focusing on God's Word may seem like a small act, but it has the power to cut through distraction and anchor us in the Unshakeable truth of His faithfulness.

The Day-to-Day Practice

Focus isn't just for the big moments—it starts in the day-to-day. We can develop the skill of focus through daily practice.

Meditating on the Word of God is one of the most powerful ways to train our focus. Choose a scripture and reflect on it for seven minutes. As you do, distractions will inevitably try to flood your mind—reminders of tasks, worries, and responsibilities. But don't let them take over. Command your mind to be still. Push past the noise and stay focused on the scripture you've chosen. This discipline will strengthen your ability to resist distractions and interruptions.

Another way to sharpen our focus daily is by learning to concentrate on one task at a time. While multitasking has its place, constantly dividing our attention can weaken our ability to focus when it truly matters.

The methods we develop in our day-to-day lives will help us in times of crisis. Consider a professional athlete who practices their sport day after day, even when there's no competition in sight. They hone their focus in routine practices, and when they step onto the field or court, their ability to concentrate under pressure becomes second nature. Similarly, when we train ourselves to focus on God's Word in everyday situations when difficulties arise, our minds instinctively turn to faith instead of fear.

This daily training prepares you for the moments that truly test your faith. In the next chapter, we'll examine how to hold onto Unshakeable focus in battle—when fear, pressure, and doubt scream for your attention.

The Power of Unshakeable Focus

Now that we've talked about building focus through daily practice, let's talk about what happens when everything is on the line—when the focus isn't just a discipline but a lifeline.

To be Unshakeable, we must develop the ability to focus intensely on God's Word. When fear and doubt try to take hold in moments of crisis, our focus must remain on God's promises—not on what we see, feel, or hear.

Mark Hankins said, "If you don't exercise authority in your thought life, you won't exercise authority in any other area of your spiritual life."

If we want to think like champions and walk in victory, we must be intentional. That means:

- Set our faces like flint on God's words—unyielding and determined, just as Jesus did when He went to the cross.
- We must make a quality decision—a firm resolve that we will not be moved.
- We must remain focused—not on the enemy's threats but on God's Unshakeable truth.

Champions don't win by accident. Great victories require great focus, whether in sports, competition, or life. To overcome the enemy, we must develop the mindset of a champion—one whose attention is firmly set on God's Word. Even in the darkest hours, when impossibility screams, our unwavering focus will lead us to victory.

To be Unshakeable—Focus!

He Will Show You

When bad news hits, it can feel like the ground shifts beneath you. But the Holy Spirit will show us things to come and prepare us before the moment arrives. Sometimes, it's a whisper, a nudge, a restlessness you can't explain. Other times, it's a sense that something's coming.

In this chapter, I want to share two stories where the Lord showed me things ahead of time. In both instances, He revealed significant things coming down the road, but I didn't recognize His leading at the time. Sometimes, we miss His promptings. But the more we learn to listen, the more we can live steady—not reactive but ready.

In the spring of 2018, I felt a vigorous stirring in my spirit that lasted for months. I didn't know its purpose or what to do with it. Looking for clarity, I called my sister to talk it through, which brought some relief. She suggested it might be lingering restlessness from preparing for a recent hotel inspection since I was the GM then. And although the inspection was over—and we had passed—the feeling still lingered.

I didn't realize then that this uneasiness was pointing to something more profound from the Holy Spirit. About a month or so later, arriving home on a Monday night after work, I got a text from my mother that read, *"Dad has been diagnosed with lung cancer..."* The report was a death sentence with only a month or so to live, as the cancer had traveled to his brain. At that moment, it all became so clear. In the restlessness for the past few months, I saw the Holy Spirit trying to show me what was ahead.

And even though the news was heavy and the kind of message no one ever wants to receive — I wasn't overtaken by fear. There was something sacred about knowing the Holy Spirit had spoken to me beforehand. It brought an Unshakeable sense of security. God knew. He saw. And He was already preparing my heart before the words ever came.

That knowledge changed everything. The storm hadn't surprised Him, which somehow gave me the fortitude to walk through it.

With any experience we have with God, it's important to remember this: we don't build our understanding of Scripture around our experiences—we interpret our experiences through the lens of God's Word. The Bible clearly says that the Holy Spirit will show us things to come.

John 16:13 says, *"Howbeit when he, the Spirit of truth, is come, he will guide you into all truth: for he shall not speak of himself; but whatsoever he shall hear, that shall he speak: and he will shew you things to come."*

A Samuel Moment

It was a Samuel moment. The Holy Spirit had been calling and stirring me into prayer, and I hadn't recognized it. In my position at the hotel at that time, I had spent many long days preparing for an inspection; it hadn't dawned on me that this stirring was from Him. If I had known, my actions would have been different, and I promised myself that would never happen again. Next time, I would recognize that leading and pray it through in the Spirit.

He will show us things to come.

Within the next few days, I flew home to Texas. While at home, Dad and I had a private conversation. When praying for someone's healing, knowing where they stand in their faith is essential. My question was simple: where was Dad in all this? Did he want to go home with the Lord, or did he want to stay here and fight? He was 83 and had lived a full life, and the road ahead was uncertain and challenging. We needed to agree. Faith will never override a person's will, so we needed to know what we believed together. If it were solely up to me, my prayers would have been for his complete healing, but his will mattered most.

Dad was a fighter. He was a man of steel and velvet. He was no lightweight, and this wouldn't be the first time we stood in faith together against the enemy. His response was clear: he was in the game, and he was going to kick the devil's butt! So, we had a plan.

But the Holy Spirit knew something I did not....

During those last six weeks before Dad went home, I visited often, flying to Texas as frequently as possible. In between visits, while I was back home in Massachusetts, my prayer life was consumed with standing against cancer and using my faith.

The Check

But often in the mornings after waking up, there would be this "check" in my spirit — a strong sense that something wasn't right. Not recognizing it as the Lord, I assumed it was the enemy and would quickly rebuke it and curse it! Yet it puzzled me because this feeling didn't come from my mind; it originated deep in my spirit. Hindsight would later reveal what it was.

Dad's health continued to decline, but my faith didn't. When you fight in faith, there is no retreat. When social workers would come into the room to discuss Dad, my response was always the same: *"You're wasting your time because my Dad is not going to die!"* The only one who had my full attention was a chaplain who graduated from the same Bible

School I had in Broken Arrow, Oklahoma. In what could only be described as divine timing, he happened to be in Texas and was now there to help us with Dad. God indeed sent him.

Despite the concerning reports and what I saw happening with Dad's health, none of it phased me. Why would it? Dad and I had always been partners in faith against the enemy's attacks, and this time was no different. He was a strong man of faith and prayer who had an intimate relationship with God and His Word.

I miss him.

The days turned into weeks; eventually, Dad just wanted to go home. He had lived a long life — over 80 years — and had a lasting impact in many people's lives. He was ready to see Jesus face-to-face after an encounter with Him just days before.

When someone decides they're ready to go home, you can't use your faith against their will. Dad had decided, but there was one problem — I was still on the battleground, believing for his healing, unaware that his desires had changed since our conversation in the back bedroom six weeks earlier. In hindsight, the Holy Spirit had been trying to tell me. But once again, I hadn't recognized it at the time.

The Cat's Claw

Hours and countless hours of praying in the Spirit became my norm during those six weeks. One night, a prominent image appeared before me in prayer — an image I can still see vividly. It was a cat's claw. Every marking, every color on that claw, was so distinct. It was lodged deep within a piece of tissue inside Dad's body — an image so detailed that it felt almost tangible.

My conclusion was simple: once that claw was removed — whatever it represented — Dad would rise from his deathbed! So, I continued to pray and press in with unwavering faith. Even as Dad's condition worsened, I refused to back down. Faith doesn't retreat, nor does it give up.

That's what Dad had taught me — to stand firm on God's Word, no matter what.

Little did I know that my last visit with Dad would be a week before he went home to be with the Lord. Before leaving for the airport, I leaned down and told him, "I'm not saying goodbye — I'll be back in a week or so."

A few days later, Mom called to tell me that Dad only had a few days left. At that moment, I knew I needed to press in through fasting and prayer. It was during a prayer meeting at church that everything became clear. The leader of the meeting, while sharing a random story, said, *"It was as if she had her claws in me!"*

Right then, the Holy Spirit spoke to me and said the words no woman of faith and power wants to hear in a moment like that:

"You, are the cat's claw."

I had told Dad during one of my visits that the Lord had shown me the cat's claw. I'd said, *"As soon as we know what the claw is, you'll be free of all this."* Little did I know that those words would come true — but in a way I had never imagined.

The Holy Spirit showed me that Dad had changed his mind. Though he had started out ready to fight, he had now chosen to go home, and I needed to release him. I had been holding on with everything in me, refusing to back down, but now it was time to let go.

For weeks, Dad hadn't been able to speak because of heavy medication. Dad wanting to go home wasn't something he could have told me — but the Holy Spirit knew, and He revealed it. Looking back, I remembered all the times the Holy Spirit tried to tell me, yet I hadn't recognized it. He knew from the start that Dad would want to go home in the end...suddenly the checks I had before clearly visible. It was the *Holy Spirit showing me.*

The lessons I learned in those six weeks are invaluable — and they all point to this truth:

The Holy Spirit will show you. Always. The Word says so.

The Leadings

Looking back, I now realize that the Holy Spirit had been alerting me — not just in the weeks following Dad's diagnosis, but long before.

Those morning "checks" in my spirit, the ones I mistook for the enemy, had been the Holy Spirit trying to get my attention. He knew I didn't know that Dad's desire would eventually change. The Holy Spirit wasn't just preparing me for the diagnosis; He guided me through the following journey, trying to let me know something. And when the time came, He revealed the most important thing — that Dad was ready to go home.

Dad went to his eternal home about a day and a half later, after the Holy Spirit showed me that he wanted to go home. Now, he's with Jesus — the one he loved so fervently — reunited with family and friends who went before him, along with the countless people he touched while here on earth. He's happy now and in the presence of perfect peace.

And within the blink of an eye, we'll see him again.

How I long for that day — to see him for eternity.

Listen to the Holy Spirit

You don't have to be caught off guard when the enemy plans to throw you off course with sudden bad news. If we stay sensitive to the Holy Spirit, we can be prepared — steady and unshaken — even in the face of unexpected storms.

The Holy Spirit is like a skilled meteorologist, warning us of approaching trouble so we can prepare and adjust accordingly. But just like a weather forecast only helps if we're paying attention, His leadings require our willingness to listen.

A consistent, disciplined prayer life—especially praying in the Spirit—sharpens our ability to recognize His voice and keeps us ahead of the game. But diligence is key.

As a hotel general manager, running the hotel had taken priority over maintaining a strong prayer life. Looking back, I now realize that my spiritual sensitivity was dulled.

Had I been more consistent in prayer, I would have recognized the restlessness I felt — the "check" in my spirit each morning — as the Holy Spirit was trying to warn me.

God's best is that we walk prepared, not blindsided. Since that season, I've learned the value of disciplined prayer — especially in the Spirit — and the peace of being sensitive to His leading.

The Holy Spirit's guidance isn't just helpful — it's essential for every believer. He will show you things to come; when He does, you can stand firm, no matter what lies ahead.

Redeemed from Not Knowing

God never intended for His children to wander through life confused or uncertain. Jesus promised us the Holy Spirit — our Comforter — who will guide us and show us things to come (John 16:13). While the world may be confused, we have an advantage: the Spirit of God dwelling within us.

The Holy Spirit doesn't leave us guessing. He directs, reveals, and brings clarity when we need it most. He will show you what to do when you are faced with a sudden report.

Uncertainty can add pressure to an already difficult situation, but we've been redeemed from the unknown as believers. We don't have to stumble in confusion. When we look to Him in those uncertain times, He will reveal exactly what we need to know.

James 1:5 reminds us of this powerful promise:

"If any of you lack wisdom, let him ask of God, that giveth to all men liberally, and upbraideth not; and it shall be given him."

This isn't just hopeful thinking — it's a guarantee. The Holy Spirit's guidance and God's wisdom are promises we can rely on. We can walk confidently when we lean into His leading, even when the path ahead seems unclear.

Darkness in the Light

One Sunday in Honolulu, Hawaii, my sister and I had just returned home from church. It was a beautiful, sunlit day that made you want to savor every breeze and all the sunshine.

We went inside to change out of our church clothes and into beachwear, eager to meet my boyfriend at Waikiki Beach. But as we walked into the apartment, something felt… off.

The living room felt unusually dark despite the bright, sunny day outside. I remember pausing, puzzled. The drapes were open, and sunlight streamed in, yet the room still seemed shadowed—heavy somehow. The furniture, the walls—everything seemed dark and muted. I even looked around to see if a light had been left off or if something was blocking the sun. But no—nothing explained it. The darkness didn't make sense.

Pushing the uneasiness aside, my sister and I changed clothes and walked down Kalakaua Avenue to the beach. We met my boyfriend at the end of Waikiki Beach.

While at the beach, my sister and I disagreed — I don't even remember what it was about now. Frustrated, she left early to walk home alone. A little while later, I followed.

What I didn't know then was that while I was still at the beach, the meaning behind that strange darkness would soon become clear — and with it, a revelation would stay with me forever.

The Attack

My sister faced one of the darkest moments of her life that day.

As she walked through the locked security doors into our apartment building, a man — someone who didn't belong there — followed her inside. He trailed her down the hallway, then stepped into the elevator behind her.

That's when he attacked.

She fought to push him away, but he was stronger. The elevator doors opened on our floor, and she bolted out, racing to our apartment with him in pursuit. He was right behind her — too close for comfort — and he lunged forward as she reached our door.

Somehow, my sister managed to open the door. But before she could fully close it, he shoved hard, trying to force his way in. With his strength against her small frame, there was no way she could overpower him. She pushed with everything she had, but it wasn't enough.

And yet...the door shut.

How?

My sister later told me an angel must have shut that door — a more potent force than her. There was simply no way she could have done it on her own.

At the time, my parents weren't home. If Dad had been there — well, things would have ended differently for that man. The police were called, and an investigation followed, but they never found him.

Looking back, I realized something important: The Holy Spirit had been trying to alert me. That darkness I had sensed earlier — the unsettling feeling that lingered despite the sunlight streaming into our apartment — was His leading. I didn't recognize it for what it was.

If I had understood then what I know now, I would have known to pray it through—to pray against whatever that darkness represented. But despite my limited understanding, God's mercy covered us. The enemy didn't get the victory that day.

The Holy Spirit will show you. Recognizing His leadings could shift the outcome. Don't ignore those nudges.

Praying in the Spirit

No words can fully describe the importance and necessity of praying in the Spirit if we want to hear clearly from Him. Praying in the Spirit sharpens our sensitivity to His leading, helping us recognize His guidance, wisdom, and strategies.

It's not just a spiritual practice — it's a powerful weapon against the enemy's tactics. Praying in the Spirit keeps us one step ahead, deflecting the fiery darts meant to throw us off guard and drag us into fear and panic.

Through the Holy Spirit, God will not only show us things to come — He will guide us, teach us, and instruct us on what to do next in battle. His leadership is a powerful tool against the enemy because God's knowledge is far greater than Satan's schemes. God has a victorious Plan B for every Plan A the enemy devises.

"I will instruct you and teach you how you should go. I will guide you with My eye." — Psalm 32:8

God's love for us is fiercely protective. His Father's heart longs to be actively involved in every detail of our lives. It's never best for us to be blindsided, overwhelmed, or thrown into panic by unexpected bad news.

The enemy may have a strategy — but God's plan always triumphs. The Holy Spirit, who dwells within us, knows the enemy's tactics and will always lead us. When we pray in the Spirit daily, we stay in step with Him.

Rest in this truth: *The Holy Spirit will show you things to come.* Trust Him, lean into His guidance, and know that He is always one step ahead, leading you to victory.

He will show you things to come so you won't be shaken when they do.

When you follow His leadings, you can confidently walk through life's uncertainties — steady, secure, and Unshakeable — knowing the Holy Spirit will always show you the way.

Unshakeable.

Jehovah Shammah

"I will go before you and make the crooked places straight: I will break in pieces the gates of brass, and cut in sunder the bars of iron." Isa 45:2

Out of every chapter, this one was my favorite to write. It speaks of God's goodness, greatness, and faithful presence—the kind of knowing that anchors you when you're staring down a bad report. While many of the other chapters are more active, this one invites you to receive—to rest in what God has already done.

When you're facing a situation that threatens to take something precious from you, nothing brings greater security than knowing that someone far greater has already gone before you—already solved the problem, already made all of the crooked places completely straight.

And yet, He's not only at the finish line—He's beside you right now.

That, my friend, is who Jehovah Shammah is and what He does.

One of the names of God is Jehovah Shammah, the God who is there. It's the final name of God revealed in the Old Testament—a powerful reminder of God's constant presence with His people.

But it doesn't end there. In the New Testament, this truth unfolds even more clearly: through the birth of Jesus—Immanuel, God with us (Matt. 1:23)—and the sending of the Holy Spirit after His ascension. Jesus said the Spirit would remain with us forever, guiding, empowering, and comforting us (John 14:16).

From the Garden of Eden, to the cross on Calvary, to your living room today—He has always been there.

And here's the beauty of it: *Jehovah Shammah is not only the God who is present with you now—He's also the God who goes before you.*

When you feel surrounded, He's surrounding you.

And when you can't see the next step—*He's already there.*

But His presence isn't just with you—it's *ahead* of you.

God is Waiting There

Why is it essential to understand that God is not only with us, but already at the finish line when we're faced with a sudden problem or a hard-hitting report?

Because when you receive an evil report, the enemy tries to paint the darkest, most hopeless picture possible. He wants the situation to look impossible, final, and overwhelming. He wants to convince you that the circumstance has the final word and that your future is determined by what's in front of you.

The darker the image, the more the enemy tries to isolate you—to make you feel powerless, trapped, and forgotten. If he can keep your focus on the problem, he can pull your attention away from the truth: God is already there at the end of the story, where victory and hope await.

But here's the good news—we are not alone.

God didn't take a nap and leave you exposed. He doesn't check out when things get messy. He's not too busy helping Aunt Susie and Uncle Henry to be with you.

Like a hotel that's open 24/7, so is God. He's with you every hour of the day. And that truth makes all the difference when bad news shows up.

But Jehovah Shammah doesn't just stand beside you in the storm—He's already ahead of you, preparing the outcome. While His presence brings comfort in the moment, it also brings confidence for the future. Because God is both with you **and** waiting for you. And that changes everything.

"So we take comfort and are encouraged and confidently and boldly say, the Lord is my Helper; I will not be seized with alarm—I will not fear or dread or be terrified. What can man do to me?" (Hebrews 13:6 AMPC)

The Power of Presence

My Dad, who is now in heaven, profoundly influenced my life. As a little girl, he was everything to me. If anything had ever happened to him while I was a child, I would have physically died. That's how deeply our connection was. That's the role he played in my life.

He was a man of steel and velvet—firm yet gentle. His love for God and people was unmistakable, and he never hid it. He loved me fiercely, and I held a special place in his heart.

Not to say that his love for my other siblings were just as equal—but Dad and I shared something unique. He taught me the ways of the Lord every single day. It often felt like it was just me, Dad, and the Lord—the three musketeers, with Jesus at the center.

Whatever Dad did, I wanted to do, wanting to be just like him.

He became a reflection of the heart of the Father God's heart for me. Because of that, I came to understand God's love through the love of my earthly father. What a gift.

As a youth, I wasn't the most popular kid at school. Being tall and thin and always wearing cute clothes, was an asset but overshadowed by the rather large physical flaws-which were targets for cruel teasing from the other kids. My teeth were very buck, my glasses changed color when I went from inside a building to outside. My naturally curly hair was impossible to tame, and back then, no one knew how to style it—so they kept it super short, and I always looked like a boy.

I wasn't good at sports, and to top it all off, my last name was "Kirk"—at the height of *Star Trek*'s popularity. You can imagine how that played out. I was easy prey for the kids who liked to mock and tease me, leaving me feeling rejected, unwanted, and odd.

But when my Dad was with me?

I felt like a queen.

Suddenly, everything was okay. His presence gave me courage, and his strength became my strength. And because I revered him so much, all that mattered was what *he* thought of me.

When he was by my side, the opinions of others faded into the background. I felt safe, shielded, and seen. The noise of the world quieted down in his presence. Looking back, I realize now that my father's presence gave me a glimpse of something far greater—what it's like to live anchored in the presence of God.

My Dad couldn't be with me everywhere. But Jehovah Shammah could.

The feeling of security and strength when my father stood beside me is only a fraction of the Unshakeable strength available when we know **God is there**—not just emotionally, but spiritually, practically, powerfully.

Dad and I weren't always together for long periods of time—and the difference with him being gone as when he was near made all the difference, especially during the hardest moments.

But there's more to this.

The Beginning and the End

God is the Alpha and the Omega—the beginning and the end. (Revelation 22:13)

That means He's not only walking with you—He's already at your finish line. He's already worked out what the enemy is trying to intimidate you with.

God never checks out, steps away, or leaves you mid-process. He's with you at the beginning of the report, the middle of the confusion, and the moment the breakthrough appears. He's Jehovah Shammah—the God who is *there* at every point.

And when He's present, victory is present.

Inside the Underneath

My brother was a big scuba diver in the past. He loved diving the Great Barrier Reef, the Cayman Islands, Hawaii…, and anywhere else he could.

Being the little sister, I decided to try it too.

I've always loved the water. Growing up in Fiji, Hawaii, and Australia, we were surrounded by it. Even now, my love is the ocean. In Fiji, we would take my dad's boat out to a nearby island, and I'd sit on the side of the boat, gazing into the water, imagining what was underneath—sharks, whales, sea snakes—all the mysterious creatures hidden below the surface.

Once, I saw a sea snake slither to the surface and dip back down again. Half in the water, half out—its slimy, oval-shaped body vanishing beneath the waves. It gave me chills. They were poisonous—and creepy.

So it was concerning when I finally went scuba diving for the first time!

The ocean was deep and dark. The water wasn't crystal clear—it was dark blue. What was I jumping into? What if a shark was circling below? What if I was the main course for dinner that night?

But the moment I jumped in, all those fears disappeared.

It was a whole other world—peaceful, quiet, and still. There were no sharks or sea snakes—just a gentle, majestic underwater world waiting to be explored.

Perhaps those creatures were out there somewhere—but they weren't near me. They weren't in view. There was only peace.

God is already there. He's in the unknown. He's in the deep. He's inside the underside. You don't have to fear what you can't see.

And when Jehovah Shammah is there, so is **peace, victory, and joy.** When the report comes and the road ahead looks dark, remember that Jehovah Shammah is already there.

With Me Wherever I Go

To further illustrate God's continual presence, Psalm 139:7–10 (AMPC) paints a powerful picture:

7 Where could I go from Your Spirit? Or where could I flee from Your presence?
8 If I ascend up into heaven, You are there; if I make my bed in Sheol (the place of the dead), behold, You are there.
9 If I take the wings of the morning or dwell in the uttermost parts of the sea,
10 Even there shall Your hand lead me, and Your right hand shall hold me.

During a particularly tough season in my life, I had a friend who had been supportive in some ways—but when I asked her to walk with me through a difficult moment, she hesitated. The situation felt too heavy for her, and though I understood her apprehension, it was hard.

That day, I realized something important: sometimes, people walk with us only when it's comfortable and convenient and not when things get too intense.

God isn't like that.

His presence doesn't have limits. He doesn't get scared or back away. He doesn't withhold His love, back out of the challenging moments, or disappear when the road gets dark.

He is Jehovah Shammah—the God who is there.

He is there in the bosses office, the waiting room, the courtroom, and the quiet car ride home. He is lovingly committed to walking with us through every moment—not just the easy ones.

When you're facing something unknown or difficult—maybe a heavy conversation, a scary diagnosis, or a decision you're afraid to make—pause and remind yourself:

God is not only with me. He is already there. He's standing at the finish line with victory in hand. I'm not alone. Not for one second.

Jehovah Shammah Is At The Finish Line

God's presence isn't just with us *right now*—He's already ahead of us. In life we can rest in the truth that God is beside us and waiting for us at the finish line. He's gone before us. The victory has already been secured.

He's mapped out your race. He knows every turn, every struggle, every unexpected moment. You may not see the full path, but He's already been there. And He's waiting at the end, cheering you on—not hoping you make it, but already declaring your victory.

It reminds me of a season when I had an assistant who constantly surprised me. I'd walk in with a long list of tasks, expecting to spend the entire day working through them. But before I could start, she'd smile and say, *"That's already done."* Again, I'd give her another task—*"That's already done."* Again and again, the same reply.

You can imagine the relief that brought! She had gone ahead of me. What I thought would be a heavy load had already been handled.

That's Jehovah Shammah.

When a bad report comes, hear Him whisper, *"It's already done."* When fear tries to rise, and the enemy says there's no way through, hear your God speak again, *"It's already done."*

He's not only with you—He's ahead of you.

When fear tries to arise, let your spirit answer boldly: He's already there and He has already made a way.

The God Who Is "There"

Let's talk about what "there" really means.

We've talked about God being at the finish line – but what is that finish line?

"There" is the place the enemy wants you to fear. "There" is where the report threatens your future. "There is the moment that looks uncertain, unstable and impossible. But "there" is precisely where *God already is.*

That's why this truth is critical to grab hold of—especially when you feel backed into a corner and don't know what to do. When fear whispers, *"You're out of time. There's no way out."* You can answer confidently:

"Jehovah Shammah is already there."

He's at the finish line in victory. He's at the place of provision. He's already gone before you to the moment of deliverance. He was there at the Red Sea, parting waters. He was there in the lion's den, keeping mouths shut. He was there in the fiery furnace, walking in the flames.

And He is there with you now—in the doctor's office, the boardroom, the bank meeting, the moment the phone rings with bad news. He is already at your breakthrough.

You may not know what to do. You may not have the answer yet. But God does.

And He is already at work.

"I will go before you and make the crooked places straight ..."(Isaiah 45:2, AMPC)

No Rooms at the Inn

I once booked a huge sports group at one of the hotels where I worked as Director of Sales. They were scheduled to arrive on a Saturday night, and we had reserved a block of rooms for them.

But on Saturday morning, while driving to a charity event in Connecticut, I got a call from the hotel's GM. Her voice was anxious. *"The team is arriving tonight... and we have no rooms for them."*

Now that, is a bad report.

The city hosted a significant event, and all the hotels were full. Where were we going to place this team? How would we explain this mess? I turned the car around and headed straight for the hotel. Fear tried to grip me. If this were my mistake, the consequences would not be pretty. But I refused to panic. I reminded myself—and the Lord—that He is the God who is **already** at the answer. He had known about this long before we did. He was Jehovah Shammah—the God who goes before me—and I clung to that truth all the way back to the hotel.

When I arrived, I looked carefully through our reservation system and double-checked every possibility. Sure enough, there were no rooms available for the group. None. But we didn't stop there. The GM and I immediately started calling around to other hotels desperately looking for enough vacancy to house this big group. Every hotel we called was completely full—until we finally found one hotel, about twenty minutes away, that could take the team for the night. The only catch? They couldn't provide breakfast.

So our team stepped in—we packed breakfast bags for the entire group and delivered them personally to the hotel. We had complete favor with not only the GM at that hotel, but also the coaches. The transition was smooth, no complaints, no chaos.

Crisis averted.

Through it all, I kept reminding myself that *God was already at the solution.* In the middle of every *what-if* and *what-if-*

not, I held on to the truth: Jehovah Shammah is there. Always.

Where do *you* need God to show up during a bad report? Where you cannot be, you need him to show up at the answer.

The solution already exists. And He is already there.

If the enemy can get us into panic and fear, he can pull us away from the truth. He'll fill our minds with pressure-filled questions like,

"What are you going to do?"
"There's no way out!"

But the truth we know is greater than the fear he tries to stir—more powerful than the questions he asks or the pictures he paints.

We used to have a cat who was basically the boss of the neighborhood. He was a fierce little hunter and constantly brought home animals that we had to rescue.

One evening, he had something *again*. I opened the front door—bracing myself—and sure enough, he ran into the foyer and dropped a mouse.

Cue the chaos.

The mouse started scurrying and squeaking, and I immediately called my then-husband for backup. We both went into full freak-out mode.

We were stumbling around, trying to catch this poor thing, yelling directions, bumping into furniture—it was a full-blown mouse-induced panic party.

And Kitty?

He just sat there.

Black and white fur, his white chest puffed out looking like he was wearing a tuxedo, not moving a muscle.

He watched us—still, calm, completely unimpressed.

You could almost hear his thoughts: *"Look at these two humans. What a show."*

While we were flailing around, Kitty had already done the hard part—he'd caught the mouse. And now, while we panicked, he just quietly observed… completely steady.

We eventually got the mouse to safety.
We were relieved.
Kitty was amused.

And I'm pretty sure we were the talk of the cat neighborhood that night.

But isn't that how we are with God sometimes?

The enemy throws a "mouse" into our lives—something small, unexpected, but chaotic—and we spiral. We panic. We speak fear. We don't know what to do. All the while, Jehovah Shammah is standing steady—unmoved, unshaken, and already holding the victory.

He sees the end we can't.

He's not pacing with us in anxiety—He's seated in peace. And He's saying, *"I'm here. I've already made a way. There's no need to panic."*

We may not see how the situation will turn out, but one thing is certain:

Jehovah Shammah is there. And that's all we need to know to hold steady—especially when all we see is nothing.

Just as Kitty was calm and perfectly positioned, *my* position at that moment was to rebuke fear, anchor myself in faith, and watch the result unfold.

Unlike the GM and me calling around for a solution, God didn't have to convene the heavenly board for an emergency meeting. He wasn't pacing the golden streets or wringing His hands saying,

"Oh no! What are we going to do? This one caught Me by surprise!"

He already had it handled. He always does.

In the Day to Day

So how do we walk with Jehovah Shammah—not just in crisis, but in everyday life?

We start by making space for Him.

Just like I got to know my dad by spending time with him, our relationship with God deepens the more we make Him a part of our daily lives. It's not about a perfect routine. It's about *intentional connection.*

Whether it's five quiet minutes in the morning, prayer time on your lunch break, or spending time with him as you wind down at night—each moment becomes a thread that weaves your heart to His. And the more we do it, the more natural it becomes, and the more we long for that time spent with Him, to the point where we will move schedules to spend more time with Him. Falling in love with Jehovah Shammah.

When uncertainty shows up—and it will—we don't panic. We don't spiral. We remember:

He is here. He is already there.

We train ourselves to lean on that truth before we lean on worry, to ask for His guidance instead of jumping into fear, and to respond with faith because we've practiced it in peace.

And over time, that awareness of Jehovah Shammah becomes part of who we are. Just look back over the past week.

How many moments looked uncertain—tight situations, last-minute changes, things you didn't expect—yet somehow, they worked out?

That wasn't coincidence. That was Jehovah Shammah.

God has always reminded His people—just like He did with the children of Israel—to *remember* what He has done.

When we recall the times He showed up—again and again— we build faith and confidence in His character.

If He's done it before, He'll do it again.

Why? Because that's who He is.

The night the hotel had no rooms for our team, this principle of Jehovah Shammah became real to me in a fresh way.

We had no plan B, no options...but God already had the answer waiting. Now, when something unexpected happens, I go back to that memory—and others like it.

God's Word is my anchor.

He's not scrambling to catch up. He's already ahead of me, working it out.

I've learned to do my part: trust Him and respond with faith. And every single time, the situation works out—because Jehovah Shammah has already gone before me.

The next time you face something unexpected—
You lock yourself out with a meeting in 30 minutes...
You get a flat tire in the rain and your phone dies...
Or you realize a customer's large credit card payment didn't go through, and they've already left...

Before panic sets in, remember Isaiah 45:2: *"I will go before you and make the crooked places straight."*

Resist fear.
Don't panic.
Reach out and lean into the One who never leaves—
Jehovah Shammah.

Because when you've seen Him in the small things, you'll trust Him in the big things. When a Red Sea moment

comes—when there's nowhere to turn but through—
remember:

He's already gone ahead of you.
We're not just reacting—we're anchored.
We're not just hoping—we're confident.
Because we know the One who goes before us.
The One who never leaves.

The One who is always, always there.

Always, Always There

We've seen what the Word says about the God who is there—right where we are and already where we're going.

Jehovah Shammah is present in the now, and He's present in the outcome.

He's not just beside you in the battle—He's already standing in the victory.

These truths stand in stark contrast to the picture the enemy paints when crisis strikes.

But when you embrace them—and practice them daily—they become the anchor of your soul.

So when fear rises, you can stand firm.

When the enemy shouts, you can stay steady.
When bad news comes, you won't be shaken.

Because Jehovah Shammah—the God who is there—has already gone before you.

And wherever *"there"* is... He is.

And that's what makes you Unshakeable.

What to Do When You Don't Know What To Do
The Hidden Benefits of Praying in the Spirit

In Tulsa, Oklahoma, directly outside what was once known as the City of Faith Hospital, stood the world's largest bronze sculpture—the Praying Hands. Towering 60 feet high and weighing 30 tons, they were an unmistakable landmark.

These hands were more than a work of art; they symbolized a life devoted to prayer. Oral Roberts, the man behind this vision, was a man of prayer. The fruit of his communion with God was evident in the impact of his healing ministry, which reached people around the globe for more than 60 years. As a televangelist, author, and founder of Oral Roberts University and the City of Faith Medical Center, his life bore witness to the power of prayer.

On the campus of Oral Roberts University, another iconic structure stands—the Prayer Tower. It's located in the center of the campus, signifying that prayer and communion with God should remain in our lives. At the top of the tower burns a continuous flame, representing the fire of the Holy Spirit and the power that comes through intimacy with Him.

Prayer is not just a discipline but a powerful tool that activates God's hand on behalf of His people. It frames our world, opens doors that seem shut, and brings answers that would never have come had someone not prayed. Scripture is filled with examples: Daniel interpreting Nebuchadnezzar's dream; Hannah's womb opening to have a son, Samuel; Daniel's deliverance from the lion's den; Peter's miraculous release from prison; and Jesus Himself—

who lived a life saturated in prayer, produced a ministry of power, healing, compassion, and wisdom.

One thing is consistent in each of these stories: Prayer brought forth divine words, deliverance, strategy, and direction in impossible situations. So, what do we do when we receive a bad report? When something throws us off course?

We pray.

Philippians 4:6 reminds us:
"Be careful for nothing, but in everything by prayer and supplication with thanksgiving let your requests be made known unto God."

While living in Tulsa, the Praying Hands were always a landmark. If they were visible while driving, it gave me a sense of where my direction was. The location was clear and I knew which way to go to get to my destination. In the same way, seeing the flame on the Prayer Tower, brought the same kind of directional security. I knew which way to go! That flame gave me clarity, just as prayer gives clarity when life feels uncertain.

And that's the power of prayer—it anchors us when life is unclear.

Just like being lost on the road, there are moments when we don't know where to turn. Moments of sudden bad news, unexpected crossroads, or overwhelming decisions. In those moments, the image of those Praying Hands serves as a reminder: if we pray, God will show us the way.

And so, it is with the Prayer Tower representing the power of prayer. Inside the tower are rooms and spaces for prayer teams—rooms set apart for intercessory prayer as well as rooms for corporate prayer. And at the top, that eternal flame burns brightly. Symbolically, a flame doesn't just represent the Holy Spirit. It represents divine knowledge, power, authority, warmth, and comfort.

And that leads us to this chapter's focus: Praying in the Spirit.

There are many forms of prayer, such as petition, thanksgiving, and intercession. Still, there is one kind that strengthens the inner man, quiets apprehension, and gives you access to the divine strategy in the middle of a crisis: praying in the Spirit.

When it feels like the walls are closing in, the pressure rises, and the way out is unclear, this kind of prayer releases the divine knowledge, power, authority, warmth, and comfort you desperately need.

The Promise and the Power

The flame atop the Prayer Tower at Oral Roberts University symbolizes more than hope—it represents the baptism of the Holy Spirit, a fire that empowers believers from the inside out.

We first read about this baptism in Acts 1, where Jesus gave an explicit instruction to His disciples:

"'Wait for the promise of the Father...for John truly baptized with water, but you shall be baptized with the Holy Ghost not many days from now.'" (Acts 1:4-5)

This wasn't just a symbolic promise but an impartation of power.

In Acts 1:8, Jesus continues:

"You shall receive power after the Holy Ghost has come upon you..."

And just as He said, that power came.

Acts 2 describes it vividly:

"There appeared unto them cloven tongues like as of fire, and it sat upon each of them. And they were all filled with the Holy Ghost and began to speak with other tongues as the Spirit gave them utterance." (Acts 2:3-4)

The event wasn't isolated – it marked the beginning of something *continual* and *personal* for every believer. What happened in the upper room wasn't just a one-time experience; it was the launching point of a new way to live and pray—with the help and empowerment of the Holy Spirit.

Praying in the Spirit is not reserved for a select few or limited to a particular denomination. It's a gift that Jesus promised, and the early church embraced. And it's still available and essential today.

When You Don't Know What To Pray

While you may not know what to do, or how to pray about a particular situation, the Holy Spirit knows. When we pray in the Spirit, we pray out God's perfect will. We join forces with the Holy Spirit who knows what and how to pray. He knows exactly what that situation needs. And when you are faced with unsurmountable odds or the outcome is not clear, you are not helpless. You can pray solutions into that circumstance through following and joining the Holy Spirit in prayer. By praying in the Spirit, you become a partner with Him.

Let's break it down real simply. Have you ever gone shopping for someone's birthday and you just don't know what to get them? You go to the mall and go to a store, and suddenly you see something and you are drawn to it, and you have such a velvety feeling about getting that particular gift for that person. You go ahead and buy it, still not knowing if they will like or need it, but the peace that you had purchasing it was so strong that you couldn't resist buying it for them. You give it to them wrapped up all pretty. They open it and gasp and say, "How did you know? I have been wanting one of these for a while now!" You didn't know, but the Holy Spirit knew what that person needed and/or wanted and and led you to it.

It's the same with prayer. You may not know what the solution is or how to even cover it in prayer. But the Holy Spirit is on top of it, He knows every solution, for every single circumstance and situation, and when we hook up with Him, like buying that gift, we can pray in the key that will unlock that door to the outcome.

I Corinthians 14:2
"For he that speaketh in an unknown tongue speaketh not unto men, but unto God: for no man understandeth him; howbeit in the spirit he speaketh mysteries."

Your Spirit joins forces with the Holy Spirit to pray out God's perfect will and plan. You may not understand what you're saying (though you *can* ask the Lord to interpret, as 1 Corinthians 14:13 says), but you are praying directly to God. It's like having a private conversation in His language—spirit to Spirit.

And here's one of the most powerful truths: *the enemy can't understand what you are praying.*

When you pray in the Spirit, it's like the CIA or FBI holding a closed-door meeting—strategizing and planning with total confidentiality. The enemy has no access to what's being said between you and God.

Praying in tongues activates God's power in the unseen realm and quiets the inner chaos in the natural realm—in your thoughts and emotions. It clears the path to hearing from God while building you up spiritually. And when your spirit is strong, it overflows into every area of your life—rising up to silence the flesh and steady your steps.

That's what *edify* means—to strengthen or build up. And in pressure-filled moments, don't we all need spiritual strengthening?

Jude 20 says:
"But you, beloved, building yourselves up on your most holy faith, praying in the Holy Ghost."

When the enemy throws his best shot—when things feel uncertain, overwhelming, or impossible, or when you don't know what to do—pray in the Spirit.

Doing so activates your spirit, where the Greater One lives. He is the strategist, the solution, the answer, the comforter, and the stabilizer. Praying in the Spirit awakens your inner man and brings your spirit to the forefront—where fear used to lead, faith now rises.

When we pray in the Spirit continually, we begin to hear God more clearly and consistently. The more clearly, we hear His voice, the easier it becomes to recognize. Then it becomes a daily rhythm –praying in the Spirit and hearing His direction. The struggle and wondering if we are really hearing from God begins to fade, because now His voice has become familiar.

And when a situation arises that catches us completely off guard, we not left scrambling for days, unsure of what God is saying or if He is speaking at all.

That's the strength of the Spirit-led life—it prepares you before the crisis ever comes.

This supernatural prayer builds your faith and strengthens your inner resolve. Faith is the weapon you'll need—not just for impossible situations but for daily victory.

Parakeet Revived: Healing at Home

After returning from a business trip to Las Vegas, I noticed something was off with my parakeet. Usually, he's chirping, flying around, and—his favorite pastime—fighting with his "friend" in the mirror. (What those two argue about, I'll never know!) But this time, he was unusually quiet. Though he ate here and there, he mostly just perched and slept.

No activity. No happy chirping. Just stillness.

It was a Saturday, so finding an avian vet was tricky. I finally got a call back from my regular avian doctor. After hearing the symptoms, her advice was immediate and serious: "You need to get him to the emergency pet hospital. This sounds urgent." She admitted it was beyond what she could treat.

I called the hospital. The estimated cost? Over $1,000.

Having gone that route before, I hesitated. Time was ticking, the pressure was mounting, and I didn't know what to do. But I *did* know the One who did know.

Instead of being ruled by fear or the moment's urgency, I chose to push back. I refused to let pressure decide for me. I turned inward to the Spirit of God within me. I needed to hear from the Lord, but first, I had to quiet my mind and the apprehension about what to do or not do.

I began to pray in the Spirit.

As I prayed for several minutes, something shifted. I didn't get a direct answer about whether to take him to the hospital—but instead, I received something greater: a surge of faith covered in authority. It was unmistakable. I knew what to do.

Quietly, I walked over to his cage. Not wanting to startle him I gently commanded healing into his little body. I spoke to every organ and bone, commanding restoration and life in the name of Jesus.

Did he immediately leap off the perch and fly around the room? No. But I stood in faith. I thanked God for healing him, shut the cage, turned on soft worship music, and let him rest.

That night, he started to move—just a little.

Each day, he grew stronger. I continued thanking God for his healing and reminding the enemy that he had no authority there. Day by day, strength returned, and soon enough, he was back to flying, chirping, and arguing with his "friend" in the mirror—healthy and a little too happy, eating more than he probably should!

Faith arose, my bird was healed, and I didn't have to spend money that wasn't in the budget.

Why?

Because I prayed in the Holy Spirit.
Because I pushed back on the pressure.
Because I chose to hear what the Spirit said to do.

That faith moved the mountain because I let God direct me and allowed His strength to rise within me.

The Moment I Let Go

When my dad was diagnosed with terminal cancer, I began flying to Texas as often as I could—weekends, weekdays, whatever it took to be with him. On one of those visits, we had to go to the hospital for a procedure, and during the drive, I had something pressing on my heart.

I had heard of an alternative doctor in the area—someone who had treated professional athletes in Houston and, according to reports, had never lost a patient to cancer. I wasn't thinking of using this doctor as the only medical route, but perhaps *in addition to* my dad's current treatment. The alternative doctor was expensive, but I didn't care.

I would have paid any price to keep my dad alive.

As I sat in the passenger seat on the way to the hospital, I began to pray in the Spirit—seeking wisdom, clarity, and answers. I quietly pressed in for at least 30 minutes, asking God what to do, to add the alternative treatment plan in or not. I had to hear from God, because He was the one who would speak to my Dad to go forward with that also.

And that's precisely what happened: *I knew what not to do.*

As soon as we arrived at the hospital, peace flooded my heart—not the kind of peace you talk yourself into—but a deep, anchored knowing: *Don't do it.* Don't pursue the alternative route. Trust the plan already in place.

Later, I would understand why. But in that moment, I trusted the peace and let go of my plan.

Over the next six weeks, I prayed in the Spirit constantly—every day and every night. It was how I stayed strong and heard from God.

When Dad entered the final stage of his journey, Mom and I would go to the hospital and sit by his side all day. He wasn't coherent—he was heavily medicated—but I'd sit by his bed, hold his hand, and just pray in the Spirit.

All day, I prayed.

The fuller story of this season is shared in another chapter called *He Will Show You*. But I can tell you this: *my faith was strong.* It was so strong that I believed that my dad would get up and walk again, even if it was gradual.

That strength came from praying in the Spirit.

But also strong were the *checks* in my Spirit along the way—those gentle, internal warnings and corrections that come when you've trained your heart to listen.

One of those came in the final stretch, as the Lord spoke to me through a phrase I'll never forget:

You are the cat's claw.

I understood exactly what He meant—I held on when my dad was ready to let go.

After weeks of praying in the Spirit, the clarity I received at that moment was undeniable.

Why This Prayer Builds Strength

Praying in the Spirit has so many benefits that it could fill an entire book—and maybe someday it will. But for *Unshakeable*, we've highlighted this type of prayer for one key reason: it anchors you. It keeps you steady—not moved by what you see, what it looks like, or what you hear—in moments of crisis.

I could write volumes on what has unfolded in my life as a result of praying in the Spirit. It's one of the most effective ways to pray. When emotions are screaming, and hopeless thoughts swirl like a storm, this kind of prayer enables you to speak directly to God—about His plan, in His language, with His wisdom. And while you're doing that, your Spirit is being strengthened and built up.

The enemy fights this kind of prayer more than almost anything else. He tries to deceive believers into thinking it's not for today—or only for the early church. But that lie is designed to strip you of one of your most powerful spiritual weapons. Why? Because praying in the Spirit helps you walk out the escape route God already prepared for you.

But like every spiritual weapon discussed in this book, it's not something we pull out for the first time during a crisis. It's something we develop in the quiet, ordinary days.

Victory doesn't begin on the battlefield—it starts in practice.

It's the day-to-day practice that prepares us for the larger battles.

If you've never been baptized in the Holy Spirit with the evidence of speaking in tongues, there's a prayer at the back of this book to guide you.

Once you receive this gift—freely given by God—begin to use it in your everyday life.

Here are some ways to start using this gift:

- Pray in the Spirit for at least 30 minutes a day
- Pray while doing dishes, cleaning, or driving to work
- Set aside time in your prayer closet to pray in the Spirit without distractions
- When you don't know what to do—pray in the Spirit
- When you feel confused or uncertain—pray in the Spirit
- When you get a devastating report—pray in the Spirit
- When you feel weary, depressed, sad, or spiritually flat—pray in the Spirit
- When facing a major decision—pray in the Spirit

Start where you are. Even five or ten minutes of praying in the Spirit is powerful. Like any muscle, your spiritual sensitivity grows stronger with daily use.

As praying in the Spirit becomes part of your daily rhythm, it will become your reflex in moments of crisis. Your Spirit will grow more sensitive to God's leading and easily recognize His peace and voice.

You'll be strengthened, edified, and built up on your most holy faith—equipped to survive life's storms and navigate daily life with wisdom, clarity, and victory.

And you will know what to do.

How Praying in the Spirit Brings Clarity and Direction

Throughout this chapter, we've discussed the power of prayer and how it anchors us in hope, confidence, and direction when we feel lost or overwhelmed. Just like the Praying Hands sculpture in Tulsa marked a direction for me, prayer centers us and points us toward God's wisdom when we're unsure of which way to go.

Praying in the Spirit is a vital part of that. It connects you to God's perfect will, builds your faith, quiets the noise, and brings clarity to chaos. Developing this kind of prayer life daily becomes your Unshakeable foundation when the winds of trouble blow.

So, whether you're facing a diagnosis, a difficult decision, or simply navigating the unknown—You'll know what to do, you'll hear clearly, and you will walk forward with Unshakeable peace and absolute confidence.

That is what it means to live **Unshakeable.**

Jurassic Park
Your Fence is Your Best Defense

Few narratives in fiction capture the imagination as powerfully as *Jurassic Park*. The iconic story, masterfully penned by Michael Crichton and brought to life on screen by Steven Spielberg, revolves around the awe-inspiring and terrifying consequences of resurrecting prehistoric creatures. While the dinosaurs are fascinating, the underlying message underscores a critical principle: maintaining the fence to keep out destructive forces.

Jurassic Park's electric fences designed to contain the dinosaurs are compromised, leading to chaos and destruction. This offers a powerful metaphor for our Christian lives. The fences were meticulously designed to ensure those magnificent yet potentially dangerous creatures remained within their designated confines. When the fences failed, the park descended into a perilous battleground. This scenario reminds us of the importance of securing our spiritual fences to guard against the enemy's attempts to steal, kill, and destroy.

John 10:10
The thief cometh not, but for to steal, and to kill and to destroy: I have come that they might have life and that they might have it more abundantly.

Christians can remain stable and secure even in the most challenging times. When life feels ferocious or overwhelming, we can stay centered on God's Word, hidden in the secret place of the Most High (Psalm 91:1), knowing that the power inside of us is greater than anything confronting us (1 John 4:4).

Psalm 91:1
He that dwelleth in the secret place of the Most High shall abide under the shadow of the Almighty.

I John 4:4
Ye are of God, little children, and have overcome them: because greater is He that is in you, than He that is in the world.

Unforgiveness

When I received a concerning letter from my doctor, my first step was to examine my heart. Was there any unforgiveness or bitterness lingering within me? Had I unknowingly left my spiritual fence open? While blaming the devil for our hardships is easy, we can sometimes give him a foothold through unresolved bitterness or resentment.

Jesus said in Mark 11:25:
And when you stand praying, forgive, if you have ought against any: that your Father, who is in heaven, may forgive you your trespasses.

Often, we think we're free of offense, yet the Holy Spirit can reveal hidden areas of resentment or bitterness. These blind spots leave our fence vulnerable. If we harbor criticism, judgment, or negativity toward others, our hearts are not aligned with God's law of love.

1 Corinthians 13:4-8 reminds us:
Love endures long and is patient and kind; love never is envious nor boils over with jealousy, It is not self-seeking; it is not touchy or resentful; It takes no account of the evil done to it. Love bears up under anything and everything that comes. Love never fails.

I once knew a woman who deeply resented her husband. Despite his profound success in his profession, she criticized him constantly, coming from a critical heart steeped in bitterness and unforgiveness. Tragically, her body developed an aggressive form of cancer. Although we prayed and believed with her for healing, her bitterness persisted, and she passed away within nine months. Her tragic story serves as a sobering reminder that anger and resentment can breach the fence, allowing the enemy to bring destruction.

While the devil exploits these breaches, we must also take responsibility for guarding our hearts. Bitterness, unforgiveness, and criticism create gaps in our fence. Even subtle feelings of hardness toward others can give the enemy access. We may think we've forgiven someone, but irritation flares within us when their name comes up. That's a signal that something is off, and we should ask the Holy Spirit for help in understanding what our heart is full of so we can change it and close any open breaches.

I was out of state for a hotel convention and had planned to meet up with a good friend for dinner—someone local to the area. She canceled abruptly without explanation, leaving me feeling rejected and hurt. I quickly told the Lord, I forgave her, but something still bothered me deep down. Days later, she sent a Christmas text with a family photo, and I intentionally ignored it, not responding. My fence was down.

When I finally sought the Lord, He showed me that the issue wasn't just her cancellation—it was my old wound of rejection being triggered. I had unknowingly allowed unresolved emotions to influence my response. When we identify these patterns, we can dismantle and replace them with love and grace.

The enemy persistently seeks entry points in our hearts. He plants thoughts of suspicion, whispers lies about others' motives, and sets up scenarios to provoke offense. If we don't recognize his tactics, we risk developing resentment and bitterness, which weaken our spiritual defenses.

Proverbs 4:23 instructs us:
Guard your heart above all else, for it determines the course of your life.

We invest in locks, security systems, and fences to protect our homes and possessions. How much more should we guard our hearts against the enemy's schemes? If we understood the lengths that Satan goes to to breach our spiritual fences, we'd take even more excellent care to secure them.

We've discussed the obvious: bitterness and unforgiveness. Now, let's look at some less obvious ways that the enemy will try to climb your fence so he can enter.

Criticism: The Sneaky Breach

A critical spirit is often a temperature gauge for our love walk—or even a sign of deep-seated resentment.

When we don't honestly care for someone, we tend to be quicker to judge them, find fault with them, or criticize their every move. Snide remarks slip out, and we justify them with thoughts like, *"Well, I'm just being honest,"* or *"Someone had to say it."*

Maybe we're technically correct—but not in God's eyes.

Isaiah 55:8 reminds us:
For my thoughts are not your thoughts, neither are your ways my way, saith the Lord.

Criticism often comes from a heart that's no longer centered on love.

Remember what our mothers used to say? *"If you can't say something nice, don't say anything."* My mom took it even further: *"If someone wants your opinion—they'll ask for it!"*

Even when you're right, you can still be completely wrong—if your heart is wrong. There have been times I thought things about someone that weren't kind—but they were true. And that's when God arrested me. One day, I was lingering on some critical thoughts about someone's behavior, and I said, *"But Lord, it's true! They really are like that!"*

He lovingly reminded me:

Love… thinks no evil. —1 Corinthians 13:5

Combined with Phil 4:8 which says-
Finally, brethren, whatsoever things are true, whatsoever things are honest, whatsoever things are just, whatsoever things are pure, whatsoever things are lovely, whatsoever things are of good report; if there be any virtue, and if there be any praise, think on these things.

God wasn't saying my observation wasn't accurate. It wasn't denial. But He was showing me that even when something is true, I don't have permission to dwell on it—especially if it causes judgment, bitterness, or self-righteousness to creep in.

We all have faults. But if we stay focused on someone else's, we create a space for resentment to grow—and that, right there, opens the breach.

Criticism is a subtle breach. It often walks right through the gate because it sounds justified. It hides behind "discernment," "truth," or "I'm just being honest." But it's still a crack in the fence. And over time, that crack weakens the structure. It disguises itself as insight or discernment, but underneath, it's often fueled by resentment and pride. Bottom line, criticism is dangerous. Keep it out.

But we keep the fence intact when we stay in our lane, guard our love walk, and think the best of others—without judgment. We keep the enemy out.

The devil doesn't need the whole gate—just a crack in the fence. And criticism can be that crack.

Political Strife

I'm not someone who watches the news every morning and night. I'll catch headlines here and there—usually while checking emails or scrolling the computer—and honestly, that's more than enough for me.

But on the rare occasion when I sit and watch the news, it doesn't take long before my heart starts to slip into strife. One story after another pulls me into frustration—what this person *did, didn't do, should do, shouldn't do*. Suddenly, I'm stirred up inside, and I'm not even sure how it happened.

Here's the thing: the news moves on—but we often don't.

Days later, we're still carrying around that same story, still "watching the news" in our minds. Then, a conversation with family or friends comes up, and someone mentions politics. Suddenly, we're passionately upset again. Words fly. Frustrations stir. It's a full-blown vent session—and strife is at the center.

And most of the time, we don't even realize it's there.

I remember one night after a ministry trip. We had just finished ministering at a church in another state and went to dinner afterward. At some point, the conversation shifted to politics. People started sharing opinions, making jokes, and airing frustrations.

As I sat there, I had a sobering thought about the people they were criticizing: These were the same people we have prayed for—asking God to give them wisdom, protection, and guidance.

It's not love to talk about, jester, or criticize leaders – we are to pray for them. Strife—even political strife—is a secret doorway for the enemy to come in. It may feel normal. It may even feel justified. But it's still strife.

The Word tells us clearly in 1 Timothy 2:1–4 to pray for all those in authority—not to rage against them in conversations or harbor offense in our hearts.

1 I exhort, therefore, that, first of all, supplications and giving of thanks be made for all men;
2 For kings, and for all that are in authority; that we may lead a quiet and peaceable life in all godliness and honesty.
3 For this is good and acceptable in the sight of God our Savior;
4 Who will have all men to be saved, and to come unto the knowledge of the truth.

So, guard your heart. Keep the fence up. Don't let political strife sneak in.

Rejection

Sometimes, the hardest person to forgive... is ourselves.

The problem is unforgiveness toward someone who hurt or offended us. But often, the deeper issue is shame—and the roots of rejection that still linger inside. We fight to let go of what *they* did, but the real struggle is how it triggered something unresolved *within us*.

Once that inner wound is dealt with, forgiveness often becomes surprisingly easy.

One day, I was out running errands when I received a phone call. The person, on the other line, was a telemarketer and after a few words, the conversation quickly turned into an argument. Tension escalated, and suddenly, he hung up on me.

I was *furious*. But deep down, I knew something more was going on.

A few days earlier, I had heard Joyce Meyer say that when something makes you angry, instead of reacting, ask the Lord, *"Why? What's really behind this?"* That came back to me in that moment.

So, I paused, prayed, and asked the Lord, *"Why am I so upset? Why does this bother me so much—especially from someone I don't even know?"*

And the Lord showed me it wasn't about the man on the phone. I was angry at *myself*.

As a child, I had often been the target of cruel jokes. Teased. Followed home. Mocked relentlessly. I never backed down from a fight—*but I couldn't fight the shame*. I couldn't fight the feeling of being rejected by the very people I wanted to be like. I wanted to be pretty like the cheerleaders, thinking I'd be loved. *Then* I'd belong. *Then* I'd be somebody.

Not being able to defend myself left me feeling powerless—and that shame followed me into adulthood.

When that man hung up on me, it didn't just feel rude—it felt familiar. It whispered, *"See? You still can't defend yourself. You're still a failure."* And in that moment, shame came rushing back.

But the Holy Spirit gently stepped in.

He showed me that my inability to fight back or lash out didn't make me less of a person—nor did it deserve the amount of shame I had placed on it.

It simply meant I had a good heart.
I didn't fight because I was weak.
I didn't fight because I was sweet, sensitive, and kind—a little girl who just wanted to be accepted, loved, and to belong.

That moment of truth set me free. Shame was highlighted and gone with the knowledge of the truth.

I thought I was angry at someone else—but the real wound was inside me. It wasn't about them. It was about how I saw myself and the secret shame I didn't even know was there.

So, if you're struggling to forgive someone or feel angry, ask the Holy Spirit to show you what's going on. It might not be about that person at all. It may be about how you've judged and shamed *yourself*. Finding the root of this brought great healing to me and allowed me to see it when other situations like this arose.

Forgiveness is a decision—not a feeling. And sometimes, the person you need to forgive most is yourself.

On the Road

If you want to test your love walk, get in the car and hit the road.

Something about traffic brings out the very thing we thought we had under control. Fast food, fast coffee, fast lanes—everyone seems to be in a race. And sometimes I wonder, *what exactly are we all rushing toward?* Is it poor time management, or is it worth risking a car crash over?

From people cutting us off to tailgaters to drivers doing 15 below the speed limit in the fast lane—nothing gets our flesh riled up quite like driving in modern traffic.

Before we know it, the *choice of words*, deep sighs, and emotional reactions emerge. Then we arrive at our destination, still worked up, retelling the story: *"Can you believe what that guy did?!"* And suddenly, what started as a frustrating moment has become a seed of **strife** lodged in our hearts.

But here's the thing: strife doesn't have to announce itself to enter—it just *settles* in quietly if we let it.

When those moments come—and they *will*—we have a choice. Let it stew… or shut the door.

Repent. Forgive. Release it. Don't let strife ride in the passenger seat of your day.

Keep the fence up. Don't let traffic—or anyone behind the wheel—drive you out of love.

Ask the Holy Spirit

No one knows our hearts better than the Holy Spirit. He sees every nook and cranny—things we've forgotten, buried, or never even realized were there.

We may think we're doing great—*"I'm fine. There's no bitterness here."* But when we invite the Holy Spirit to shine His light, we're often surprised by what comes up.

I remember asking Him to show me anything in my heart that needed healing or release. And to my surprise, memories surfaced—things I hadn't thought about in years. But those old moments still held a charge in my heart. They were open doors I needed to close through forgiveness.

I'm not saying we need to dig through every moment of our past. We don't need to go on a hunt. But when we ask, the Lord will show us what needs attention. He'll highlight the places where strife, unforgiveness, or bitterness is trying to settle or has settled so we can shut the door and guard the fence.

Conclusion

When we walk in love, we maintain a strong, unbroken fence, choosing forgiveness, compassion, and humility.

That fence becomes a spiritual defense system. Knowing we've secured our spiritual borders enables us to face sudden challenges or unexpected news with peace, confidence, and clarity.

Like a locked door keeps a thief from walking in, a guarded heart **denies the enemy access.**

Keep your fence up. Keep your heart clean. And when pressure comes, you'll be able to say with boldness:

My fences are up, and my heart is whole. "No weapon formed against me shall prosper..." (Isaiah 54:17)

This is how we live Unshakeable:
By repairing what's been broken.
By watching the gates.
By recognizing the breaches before the enemy slips through.

When we stay alert, stay in love, and stay full of truth, the enemy may come knocking—but he won't get in.

Your hedge stays up. Your heart stays strong. And you stay Unshakeable.

Don't wait until the raptor's in the kitchen. Patch the fence. Guard the gate.

Stay Unshakeable.

Peace When Everything Falls Apart

I stretched out my hand to shake the newly hired manager's hand, but her calm demeanor contrasted with my enthusiasm. At first, I assumed she was just nervous on her first day, but I soon discovered otherwise.

After observing her for several months, I realized I had misread her calmness. It wasn't due to nerves—it was just who she was: steady. I watched her in high-pressure situations, leading her department with the most employees in the company. With more people came more challenges—challenges those other managers rarely faced.

Yet, she remained calm when employees or clients were angry and shouting. She would stand firm, looking the upset person straight in the eye, poised and composed when other managers would have been intimidated. Her quiet confidence and unwavering presence diffused tense situations, bringing a sense of control.

That steady assurance reminded me of the peace God offers us, a peace that can anchor us no matter what storm rages around us. When we face sudden bad news, God's peace can keep us steady, like the manager above, anchored fearlessly in the eye of the storm with hope and confidence.

"...in quietness and confidence shall be thy strength...Isa 30:15

The Eye of The Storm

In any hurricane or cyclone, the "eye" is the calm center surrounded by raging winds and violent pressure systems. Chaos spins dangerously close, but the eye remains untouched by the storm's fury. No matter how fierce the storms become, they can't break into the eye unless that calm center shifts and joins the chaos. Inside the eye, no rain falls. The winds fall silent. The air is clear and still, even as destruction surrounds it. It's not the absence of a storm-it's peace in the middle of it.

Metaphorically, this is where we want to dwell during life's storms. Chaos may threaten to uproot and overwhelm us, but we can remain in the eye of the storm, shielded in God's peace. Bad news may rage, but it doesn't have to rage within us.

The Peace of God

Jesus knew his disciples would face trouble, so He promised them peace, unlike anything the world could offer. He states in John 14:27: *"Peace I leave with you, my peace I give unto you: not as the world giveth, give I unto you."*

The peace Jesus offers is distinct from what the world offers. His peace provides Unshakeable security even when fear and destruction try to overtake us. Unlike the world's fragile peace, His peace is anchored in the truth that God is for us, so who can be against us? This peace secures us in hope and faith, no matter how dark the situation may seem.

Philippians 4:6-7 describes this powerful peace:
6 Be anxious for nothing, but in everything by prayer and supplication with thanksgiving let your requests be made known unto God.
7 And the peace of God, which passeth all understanding, shall keep your hearts and minds through Christ Jesus.

"Keep" means to guard, like a soldier standing watch. God's peace acts as a protective barrier over our hearts and minds, shielding us from anxiety.

Peace is an undisturbed state of mind that comes from within and is not dependent on circumstances. It empowers us to remain calm when chaos swirls. It's an inward assurance that we are safe and secure no matter how dark the storm appears. God's peace shields us like the calm eye of the storm.

God's Peace in the Storm

The disciples experienced this power firsthand:

Mark 4:37-39
37 And a great storm of wind arose, and the waves beat into the ship, so it was now complete.
38 And he was in the hinder part of the ship, asleep on a pillow: and they awake him, and say unto him, "Master, carest thou not that we perish?"
39 And he arose, and rebuked the wind, and said unto the sea, "Peace, be still." And the wind ceased, and there was a great calm.

The Sea of Galilee was known for sudden, violent storms. Despite the raging wind and waves filling the boat, Jesus remained asleep in the stern—the area of control and direction. He rested so profoundly that even the crashing waves didn't wake Him. The disciples, however, were panicking—the winds were so strong that they threatened their balance while trying to maintain control of the boat, with water rising quickly and the boat beginning to sink.

But when the disciples roused Jesus, he calmly rebuked the wind and commanded, "Peace, be still." Instantly, the storm ceased, and a great calm followed. Peace was Jesus's lifestyle. He remained unshaken by threats, bad news, or unexpected storms. Nothing caught Him off guard or pulled Him from His place of calm assurance. Jesus was Unshakeable.

1 John 4:17 declares, "*As He is, so are we in this world.*" That same Unshakeable peace is available to you. Whether you are facing a frightening diagnosis, a financial setback, or overwhelming grief, you can remain anchored in God's peace. Here's what you can do right now to stay in the eye of the storm:

Rebuke Fear: Fear is a thief – it will try to rob you of peace and cloud your judgment. Speak to fear the way Jesus spoke to the storm – with authority. Command it to leave in Jesus' name.

Feed on God's Word Daily: Peace comes from knowing God's Word. God's promises are your anchor. Find scriptures that speak to your situation and hold onto it like a lifeline.

Keep Your Mind on Those Promises, Not on the 'What-Ifs': Worry thrives on worst-case scenarios and robs you of your peace. When your thoughts spiral, redirect them back to what God has said. Isaiah 26:3 reminds us, "*You will keep him in perfect peace whose mind is stayed on You.*"

Yield to the Peace on the Inside: God's peace isn't something you have to fight for—it's already within you. The Holy Spirit, your Comforter, is your ever-present source of calm.

Pray in the Spirit: Get in touch with that peace that dwells on the inside by praying in the Spirit. It will bring forth God's peace and still the enemy's influences of despair.

Practicing Peace

Practicing peace begins in our daily lives. Each day presents opportunities to maintain our peace—traffic delays, difficult conversations, or unexpected challenges. We must choose peace intentionally, casting our cares on the Lord and trusting Him to work things out.

To walk in the peace Jesus promised in John 14:27, we must obey His instruction: *"Let not your heart be troubled."* Peace is available, but it requires intentional practice. We cultivate peace in the ordinary moments so that when storms arise, we naturally stand firm in calm assurance.

Peace isn't passive. It's a choice not to enter the chaos. When everything around you is swirling, the temptation is to react, to panic, to engage the storm. But you don't have to join the chaos. Staying in peace is how you stay in position—rooted, anchored, unshaken.

The storm may be fierce, but you are not in it. Whether you picture yourself in the calm eye of the storm or surrounded by a fortress-unshaken, unmovable – the truth remains: God's peace is right there with you.

His peace isn't fragile; it's fierce, powerful, and stronger than the storm. No matter what storm surrounds you, God's peace is more remarkable.

You are held steady in his perfect calm, not at the mercy of the winds. Peace is your anchor, your strength, and your weapon. Storms may come, but they don't have the final say—**God's peace does.**

So, stand firm, rebuke fear, and hold onto his promises; peace will keep you steady, confident and assured. Like Jesus in the boat and the calm manager at work, we can experience its powerful results when we stay in peace.

Stay in peace, don't join the chaos, and you'll remain Unshaken.

You've Got the Victory
Break Free From What is Blocking It

Understanding your identity in Christ is not just important, it's powerful and necessary—especially in times of trouble. It's your shield of authority against the enemy's assaults.

Bad reports and sudden changes are designed to shock, intimidate, and make us feel powerless. Whether it's our health, finances, family, or future, the pressure of the crisis tries to convince us that it holds all the power.

But it doesn't. And it never did – for those who are in Christ and know it.

The title of this book is *Unshakeable*. Part of being Unshakeable is knowing you already have a firm foundation and refusing to be moved from it.

In this chapter, I want to explore a few of the most common thought patterns that arise in times of trouble—misconceptions that block us from walking in the victory we already have in Christ.

We'll confront these lies with truth—God's Word and our identity in Him.

Because when you don't know who you are in Christ, these misconceptions can keep you trapped—shaken, defeated, and under the influence of the enemy's schemes.

And when something hits that tries to throw you off balance—one of your greatest weapons is the reminder:

"I already have the victory."

Our first reaction in a crisis is fear, passivity, or surrender. But God has already made you victorious in Christ.

You're not waiting for victory—you're walking in it.

Still, if you don't know who you are, you'll be more vulnerable to the enemy's lies—and those lies will talk you out of your authority.

"If you faint in the day of adversity, your strength is small."
— Proverbs 24:10

So, what weakens our strength?

A battle demands strength—especially strength above the enemy. But if we cling to false information or internalize lies, we're already at a disadvantage. Misconceptions quietly drain our courage, leaving us too weak to stand when it matters most.

Every spring, I love buying flowers to put on my window shelves. It's one of my favorite seasonal traditions—the blooms bring such color and life, especially on warm, sunny days.

But last year, something went wrong.

My flowers began to die, and I didn't understand why. I hadn't changed my watering schedule; the sun exposure was the same, and this type of flower had never given me any trouble.

Then, one day, I looked closer. Tiny white spots covered the stems. I Googled it—and sure enough, those spots were actually tiny insects. They weren't visible at a glance. But they were there. And they were slowly drinking all the water out of the plant—draining the very life it needed to survive.

That's what misconceptions do. They're like tiny lies that cling to the truth—but drain it. They may not look dangerous at first but left unchecked; they slowly weaken your ability to stand. They suck the life out of your confidence. Your joy. Your victory.

Check the roots if you're constantly afraid, overwhelmed, or discouraged.

Ask yourself: *What am I believing right now?*

Let's look at three common misconceptions that sneak in during crises and steal the truth of who you are in Christ. For each one, let's replace the lie with what God *really* says.

Misconception #1: "God is Sovereign" (So I Don't Need To Act)

One of the most common things you'll hear during a crisis is this phrase: *"Well, God is sovereign."*

It's usually said to suggest that whatever happens must be God's will—because He controls everything. So, if we go through a significant loss, an attack, or a devastating trial, we chalk it up to God's sovereignty. We resign ourselves to the outcome. We say things like:

- *"Well, I guess God allowed it."*
- *"If He wanted it to happen, it would have happened."*
- *"If He didn't stop it, it must be His will."*

But let's be clear: this is not biblical sovereignty.

Yes, God is sovereign. But what does that mean?

It means He is supreme in power, excellence, and position. But nowhere in the biblical definition does it say that God micromanages every outcome or overrides human will and responsibility.

The entire storyline of the Bible proves the opposite of this misconception.

- Adam and Eve made a choice.
- Israel made choices.
- We make choices every day.

If God controlled everything, there would be no such thing as free will, sin, rebellion, repentance, or redemption.

God's sovereignty does not cancel out our responsibility.

He has given us power and authority to act—to believe, to resist the devil, to choose life or death, blessing or cursing (Deut. 30:19). And when we believe the lie that "whatever happens is just God's will," we hand over our authority, sit down in surrender, and allow the enemy to wreak havoc unchecked.

But Jesus was clear:

"The thief comes only to steal, kill, and destroy; I have come that they may have life and have it to the full."— John 10:10 (NIV)

If it steals, kills, or destroys—it's not from God. And if it's not from God, you don't have to lie down and take it.

The Truth:

God has given you a role to play. He's given you authority, voice, and power. You are not powerless. You are not a passive participant in your own life. You are an active co-laborer with Christ.

Who You Are in Christ:
- You have been given authority over all the power of the enemy (Luke 10:19).
- You are seated with Christ in heavenly places (Ephesians 2:6).
- You are a joint heir with Jesus (Romans 8:17).
- You have been given everything you need for life and godliness (2 Peter 1:3).

You are not a spiritual bystander. You are a warrior positioned for victory.

Misconception #2: "God Is in Control" (So I Just Have To Accept It)

This is another misconception that often gets repeated—especially during pain or uncertainty.

"Well, God is in control..."

It sounds comforting at first. But behind that phrase is a dangerous assumption: If God is in control, everything that happens must be part of His plan. And if everything is part of His plan, then I don't need to stand, resist, or fight back. I need to accept it—because God must be doing it.

This belief causes people to relinquish their rights to stand on God's promises. It sounds spiritual, but it's spiritual passivity in disguise.

Let's ask the tricky question: If God is in control, what exactly is He controlling? Look around. The world is in chaos. There's destruction, injustice, sickness, abuse, corruption, violence. Is God *controlling* that?

Absolutely not.

God is not the author of evil. He is not orchestrating tragedy to teach you something.

He's a good Father. And good fathers don't break their children's legs to teach them how to walk.

Here's the real deal: Satan is called *"the god of this world"* (2 Corinthians 4:4). That's why the world looks the way it does. It's not under God's complete rule—not yet.

But for believers? Something radically different is true.

"[God] has delivered us from the power of darkness and has translated us into the kingdom of His dear Son." Colossians 1:13 (KJV)

We've been pulled out of the dominion of darkness. We no longer live under the control of the enemy or the curse of this world. We've been transferred into a new kingdom—God's kingdom—and that kingdom lives inside us. Yes, one day we'll be in heaven, where God reigns in full, visible sovereignty—and it will be glorious. No more pain, no more sorrow, no more death. But until that day comes, we're still living in a fallen world, and we have a role to play. We carry His authority here and now, and we've been given the victory to enforce it.

If we believe that God is in control of everything, we'll start attributing the enemy's works to God's character. We'll begin to think God "gave us" sickness. That He "allowed" disaster. He's withholding deliverance because it's somehow holy.

And we'll sit down and do nothing—just like the enemy wants. But when you realize that God is not controlling evil, you are free to stand against it.

The Truth:

God is not putting destruction on you—He's delivered you from it. He's not the one controlling the mess around you. Instead, He's given you authority in the middle of it. You don't have to passively accept what the enemy throws your way. You've been empowered to resist, to speak the Word, and to walk in victory—right in the midst of the storm.

Who You Are in Christ:

- You are no longer under the control of darkness (Colossians 1:13).
- You are a citizen of heaven (Philippians 3:20).
- You are equipped with spiritual weapons to tear down strongholds (2 Corinthians 10:4).

- You are called to resist the devil—and he will flee from you (James 4:7).
- You are not powerless—you are victorious in Christ. (I John 5:4)

Misconception #3: "Que Sera, Sera" (Whatever Will Be, Will Be)

The popular song from the 1960's, *"Que Sera, Sera,"* may have had a beautiful melody, but its message has quietly made its way into the hearts and minds of many believers. The idea that *"whatever will be, will be"* sounds poetic... even peaceful.

But when this thinking shows up in the middle of a spiritual battle, it becomes paralyzing. When people adopt this mindset, they stop fighting, believing, and standing.

They wait for the storm to pass, saying things like:

- *"Whatever happens, happens."*
- *"God will work it out if He wants to."*
- *"I'm just hoping to make it through somehow."*

They often quote Romans 8:28:
"All things work together for good..."

But that's not the whole verse.

"...to those who love God, to those who are the called according to His purpose."

There is a partnership implied. Love. Calling. Purpose. Participation.

We're not waiting on God—God is waiting on us.

When we sit back with a "whatever will be, will be" attitude, we unintentionally surrender our authority and open the door for the enemy to operate freely. The result may still be *something*, but it won't be what God intended. It will be what we allow.

God has a rescue plan for every area of your life. But that plan requires your participation.

Faith is never passive.
Faith acts.
Faith speaks.
Faith resists.
Faith moves.

Jesus already won the victory. But now, it's up to us to enforce it.

"Submit yourselves therefore to God. Resist the devil, and he will flee from you."
— James 4:7

That's not passive. That's a fight. God has given us weapons. His Word. Prayer. Praise. Authority. He's given us the right to speak to mountains, resist the enemy, pray in the Spirit, rejoice even in trial, and stand firm on His promises. It's far from *que sera, sera*. It's *"....having done all to stand—stand therefore."* (Ephesians 6:13–14)

And in all these misconceptions, we see the same underlying trap: passivity.

But we've been given power and authority. We are not waiting for God to take over. He already has—through Jesus. Now, we're called to *enforce* what's already been won.

The Truth:

Jesus has already done everything needed for your victory. The cross was not partial. It was total.

God is not holding back—He's equipped you to take the land. You're not powerless. You're not helpless. You are in Christ—and in Christ, you've already won.

Who You Are in Christ:

- You are more than a conqueror (Romans 8:37).
- You are a co-laborer with God (1 Corinthians 3:9).
- You have the mind of Christ (1 Corinthians 2:16).
- You are strong in the Lord and in the power of His might (Ephesians 6:10).
- You are not the tail—you are the head (Deuteronomy 28:13)

You are no longer in the enemy's kingdom. You are in Christ—and Christ has already won. You're not fighting for victory. You're fighting from it.

There's no room for passivity in the winner's circle.

Conclusion:

Winning on the day of battle begins with one critical truth: You've already won.

When despair, anxiety, or worry try to rise against you, you don't fight for victory—you stand in it. You are more than a conqueror. You are not the victim of the battle—you are the victor in Christ.

Psalm 18:29 says, *"With my God, I can run through a troop, and by my God, I can leap over a wall."*

In other words, with God, there's no obstacle too strong and no enemy too great. To walk in that kind of strength, you must know:

- Who you are
- Who you are not
- Who God is
- And who God is not

God is not working with the enemy to harm you. He is not indifferent, distant, or using destruction to teach you a lesson. He is a good Father on your side, providing your escape and securing your victory.

Knowing that you already have the victory means you can reject any belief that says:

- "God caused this…"
- "God allowed it…if He wanted it to happen, it would have happened…"
- "God orchestrated this…"
- "God will do what He wants, no matter what I do…"
- "Whatever happens, happens, God is in control…"

Because those beliefs lead to passivity, passivity hands your authority right over to the enemy. That's what Adam and Eve did. But that's not what you're going to do. You were made for more. You've been given authority, identity, and power in Christ. You've been seated with Him. The enemy has already been defeated.

Now is the time to enforce that victory.

To Be Unshakeable:
Know who you are. Know whose you are. And know that you've already won.

Victory Confession:
I am not a victim.
I am seated with Christ.
I have power, authority, and the mind of Christ.
I resist the devil, and he must flee.
I already have the victory—because I am in Christ!

Hold On and Let Go

Thank you for reading *Unshakeable*.

My hope is that this book has encouraged you, brought you a few laughs, and most of all—challenged you to live a life rooted more deeply in God and His Word.

You may be walking through incredibly tough times right now. If so, I encourage you: *hold on to God and His Word.* Let go of fear, dread, panic, and apprehension. Hold on to the truth that God loves you fiercely.

If you're a born-again child of God, you have rights. You have a covenant. You have the Holy Spirit living on the inside of you. You have peace, you have wisdom, and you have access to everything God has already provided for you.

When we understand the depth of God's love for us—and all that Jesus has accomplished on our behalf—we stop being tossed by the enemy's threats. We stop being intimidated by what he's tried to plan against us. Instead, we stand firm. We become rooted.

God loves you!

We live steady—not swayed by the day, not defeated by the darkness.

We live grounded in God's Word, His promises, and His love.

Unshakeable people are a threat to the enemy.

And because of *Who* is within us, we are stronger than anything that comes against us.

So, remember:

God loves you. Hold on to Him and His Words above all else.

And enjoy the Unshakeable life.

Prayer To Receive Jesus as Your Lord and Savior

Heavenly Father, I come to You in the Name of Jesus. Your Word says, "Whosoever shall call on the name of the Lord shall be saved" (Acts 2:21). I am calling on You. I pray and ask Jesus to come into my heart and be Lord over my life according to Romans 10:9-10: "If thou shalt confess with thy mouth the Lord Jesus, and shalt believe in thine heart that God has raised him from the dead, thou shalt be saved. For with the heart man believeth unto righteousness; and with the mouth confession is made unto salvation." I do that now. I confess that Jesus is Lord, and I believe in my heart that God raised Him from the dead.

I am now reborn! I am a Christian—a child of Almighty God! I am saved! You also said in Your Word, "If ye then being evil, know how to give good gifts unto your children: HOW MUCH MORE shall your heavenly Father give the Holy Spirit to them that ask him?" (Luke 11:13). I'm also asking You to fill me with the Holy Spirit. Holy Spirit, rise up within me as I praise God. I fully expect to speak with other tongues as You give me the utterance (Acts 2:4). In Jesus' Name. Amen.

If you have prayed this prayer, welcome to the family of God. If you were to die today, you can be assured of eternal salvation, forever and ever. I have a small book that I would love to send you. You can email me at kathykirkministries@gmail.com with your information of where to mail it.

And remember, God Loves *You!*

Prayer To Receive The Holy Spirit

My heavenly Father, I am a believer. I am Your child, and You are my Father. Jesus is my LORD. I believe with all my heart that Your WORD is true. Your WORD says that if I will ask, I will receive the Baptism in the Holy Spirit, so in the Name of Jesus Christ my LORD, I am asking You to fill me to overflowing with Your precious Holy Spirit. Baptize me in the Holy Spirit. Because of Your WORD, I believe that I now receive, and I thank You for it. I believe that the Holy Spirit is within me and, by faith, I accept it. Now, Holy Spirit, rise up within me as I praise my God. I fully expect to speak with other tongues as You give me the utterance.

Meditate on these scriptures about the Holy Spirit:
Luke 11:9-13;
John 14:10, 12, 16-17;
Acts 1:8, 2:4, 32-33, 38-39, 8:12-17, 10:44-46, 19:2, 5-6;
1 Corinthians 14:2-15, 18, 27;
Ephesians 6:18; Jude 20.

If you would like more on this topic, I will send you a small book. Please email me at kathykirkministries@gmail.com and provide a mailing address for us to send it to.

Acknowledgments

To my pastor, Graham Jones, for encouraging me to write a book, not a pamphlet! Your support and guidance helped shape the direction of this project, and I'm truly grateful.

Thank you to those who supported me through this journey—especially the friends who were patient when I couldn't show up or be available as much as I wanted to.

Thank you to those who encouraged me, even in small ways, when I needed it most.

Writing this book has been a deeply personal and faith-filled journey. During the writing of this book, my own faith has been challenged and I too have had to practice the principles written herein. Other times, it was extremely frustrating. But in every moment, God was with me—guiding, strengthening, and bringing the words I didn't know I had. To Him be all the glory. This is His book, written through this honored vessel.

To every future reader walking through the pages of *Unshakeable*: thank you for letting me speak into your life. May you rise stronger, steadier, and more grounded than ever before.

About the Author

Kathy Kirk is an ordained minister, speaker, and faith-filled encourager. She has traveled domestically and internationally ministering through music, teaching, and preaching, and currently serves in her local church and its affiliated ministries. With a passion for helping others grow strong in God's Word, she shares messages that are bold, compassionate, and full of hope. *Unshakeable* is her first book.

For speaking engagements or inquiries, contact her at:
kathykirkministries@gmail.com

Visit my website at kathykirk.org

www.ingramcontent.com/pod-product-compliance
Lightning Source LLC
Chambersburg PA
CBHW020927090426
42736CB00010B/1059